The Art of **Bird Identification**

The Art of Bird Identification

PETE DUNNE

featuring illustrations by David Gothard

STACKPOLE
BOOKS

To the ones who teach the "Introduction to Birding" courses,
lead the Saturday morning bird walks, write the weekly
newspaper columns, post the sightings, and pen the blogs . . .

To the mentors. Bird watching's ambassadors.

Copyright © 2012 by Pete Dunne

Published by
STACKPOLE BOOKS
5067 Ritter Road
Mechanicsburg, PA 17055
www.stackpolebooks.com

Printed in the United States

10 9 8 7 6 5 4 3 2 1

First edition

Color illustrations by David Gothard
Silhouettes in chapter 3 by Luke Seitz
All photos by Pete Dunne/Linda Dunne unless otherwise noted

Library of Congress Cataloging-in-Publication Data

Dunne, Pete, 1951–
  The art of bird identification / Pete Dunne ; featuring illustrations by David Gothard. — 1st ed.
     p. cm.
  ISBN 978-0-8117-3196-6
  1. Birds—Identification. I. Title.
  QL677.5.D844 2012
  598.01'2—dc23
                                   2012005464

Contents

Introduction:
A Revelation

"**A**ctually," I said to Kenn Kaufman, "bird identification bores me." Kenn's response was no response. In fact, his face went blank.

With shock.

We were on a trail near a lodge on the Napo River in Peru. We were between encounters with some of the neat endemic birds of the Amazon rain forest and, in the manner of colleagues, talking shop—which in the case of bird watching, almost inevitably comes around to the subject of bird identification. This should surprise no one.

As subjects go, the ability to distinguish one bird species from the next is fundamental to birding. And standing together on the trail that morning were two of the architects of modern bird identification: Kenn, whose *Field Guide to Birds of North America* deserves to be in every new birder's hands, and me, who wrote with coauthors David Sibley and Clay Sutton *Hawks in Flight*, a book which many say changed the way birds are looked at, as well as an *Essential Field Guide Companion* that imparts the identification hints and clues basic field guides don't have room for.

You can see why my disclosure shocked the normally implacable Kenn.

It probably shocked you, too. "Why," you must be wondering, "would anybody who considers bird identification *boring* write a book on the subject?"

My answer is: "Maybe that is precisely why—and why this book is going to differ in its approach." If all you want to do is pin a name to a bird, buy and use a field guide. But if you are serious about birding, if you want to learn a *skill set* you can apply to the identification of *all* birds, stationary and in flight, near and far, then read this book.

But *boring?* OK, maybe I'm exaggerating. What I should have said was that there was a time in my evolution as a birder that I found identification tedious. Back when the way we were told to distinguish one species from the next was by piecing together individual bird parts.

Me? I prefer looking at *whole* birds, not just parts. Noting, of course, textbook field marks but also and simultaneously integrating all the other manifest hints and clues that distinguish *this* bird from *that* one. Size, shape, posture, movements, mannerisms . . . I also like looking at birds as elements within their environments, not specimens taken by selective focus out of context.

This holistic approach to identification—one that focuses on the big picture first and details last—is natural and time tested. In fact, it predates "modern" bird watching. It integrates fundamental techniques that have served birders since the beginning and insights

If all birds were as easy to identify as this male Hooded Merganser, you would hardly need this book.

and shortcuts that have pushed the frontier of field identification to the limits of human perception.

And it is hardly my invention. Go back to some of the first books written about field birding and you will find many of the elements presented in this book already codified.

But these seminal treatments are long out of print, and you didn't start birding in 1889. You're starting now, and while birding's basic principles have not changed, the knowledge and skill base of birding has. Now more than ever it is important to start "learning your birds," as my mentor used to say, by getting off on the right foot.

But it's also important to follow through with your left foot—to approach the challenge of bird identification in a way that brings every advantage to bear.

So why does bird identification bore me? For the same reason you are beginning to get bored with this introduction. Because you aren't interested in learning about bird identification, you are eager to learn how to do it.

Fair enough. You begin by turning the page.

1 | Leap of Faith

We were leading a birding workshop group through Higbee Beach Wildlife Management Area in Cape May, New Jersey. The "we" consisted of me and my coleaders, Pete Bacinski and David Sibley. The group was two dozen birders of varied skill. Some were beginners, some accomplished. All had come to advance their identification skills—including a retired librarian who very apparently had Missouri blood flowing in her veins and who, having recognized the future author of *The Sibley Guide to Birds* as the youngest member of our group, took it upon herself to put David under the character-building yoke of her unbridled skepticism.

About midmorning, midweek, David looked skyward and announced: "There's a flock of Snow Geese." And so there was. Framed against a perfect autumn sky, an iconic wedge of migrating waterfowl.

"OK, David," the librarian challenged, "how do you know they're Snow Geese?"

Showing characteristic patience, David began enumerating the distinguishing characteristics—the lines of differentiating fact and circumstance that cross over a single species.

The trick, of course, is perceiving these clues correctly and recognizing their significance—another way of saying "if you don't know what you are looking at, then you need to know what to look for and how to look for it."

Hmm. They're big, long-necked, short-tailed, pointy winged birds that are all white with black wing tips. Does anybody see anything about these birds that is inconsistent with the identification Snow Geese?

"Well," he began, "they're big. And they have long necks, short tails, and long, pointy wings. And they're all white with black wing tips. And they're in a large flock, flying in a V."

He stopped. Confident that while not exhaustively complete, his enumeration of manifest traits was as sufficiently supportive as his diagnosis was unassailably true. He was wrong.

"I can see all that, David," the librarian informed him. "But what I want to know is how can you tell they're *Snow Geese*?"

David opened his mouth to speak . . . but closed it over the unspoken thought.

He tried again to formulate a response, but this utterance, too, never passed his lips. I have no idea what thoughts were cascading like bumper cars along the gyri and sulci of one of the planet's most analytical minds. All I can say is that, trapped in a metaphysical gridlock, David simply stood there, frozen in a paradoxical headlight.

How *do* you respond when someone calls into question the most fundamental tenets of your faith? That what a bird is and what it looks like are one. In this case, that birds that look and behave like Snow Geese are going to be Snow Geese.

And what do Snow Geese look like? They look like big, long-necked, short-tailed, pointy-winged birds that are all white with black wing tips and fly in a big V-shaped flock.

Just like David said.

The Basic Tenets of Bird Identification

Before proceeding, there are certain fundamental tenets of bird identification that you, as a birder, must accept on faith.

Repeat after me:

1. There is not only one bird. There are multiple species—in fact, across the planet, about ten thousand of them.
2. Each bird species is genetically distinct from all others.
3. The distinctive traits that are unique to a species are shared by every member of that species.
4. This species-specific uniqueness manifests itself in how birds appear and behave.
5. These distinguishing characteristics can be noted in the field and, when noted correctly, can be used to distinguish one species from the rest.

There in an eggshell are the underscoring principles of field identification. And yes, they do seem obvious and unassailable—hardly worth mentioning in a book. Except that not long ago, this was not the case. Field identification is a relatively new art.

Big Bang Theory

Until the end of the nineteenth century, there was no such thing as "bird watching." The study of birds was a science, called ornithology, and the primary tool of ornithologists was the shotgun.

As an instrument of study, the shotgun is limited. Bring a fowling piece to your shoulder. Train it on a perched Ivory-billed Woodpecker. The bird looks just about the way it looked with the gun at your side but . . .

There are about ten thousand bird species apportioned across the planet. Some are widespread; others, like this male Lesser Prairie-Chicken, are more geographically restricted.

BANG!

Pull the trigger. Dust the bird with shot. Retrieve it. You'll note a transforming world of difference.

Yes, the bird is dead. Not the transformation I'm speaking of.

The bird is transformed by proximity. You can now see every detail, every feather, every consolidating nuance that links the Ivory-billed Woodpecker to all the other members of the scientific order Piciformes and the family Picidae and the genus *Campephilus* and, finally, the idiosyncratic differences that distinguish *Campephilus principalis* from all other woodpeckers, making it a unique species.

Most of the traits used by scientists to group, distinguish, and name species related to structure and plumage characteristics. To this day, some of the traits used in the naming of some species cannot easily be noted unless the bird is in the hand—traits like the "sharp shin" on a Sharp-shinned Hawk or the "orange crown" on an Orange-crowned Warbler.

One of the advantages inherent in collecting birds was the enduring element it conferred. Encounters in the field are momentary. Now you see the bird, now you don't. But collected and rendered into a study skin—i.e., skinned, stuffed with cotton, preserved popsicle-style with the beak forward, wings folded, and a stick protruding from its posterior—a bird presents distinguishing characteristics that can be noted, at leisure, over and over again.

When they were not being studied, these birds were stored in specimen trays and drawers, which were usually filled with other representatives of the species and closely related species. Open the drawer. Withdraw the bird. Note its distinguishing characteristics. Pin the name to the bird.

So how did the "shotgun school" of bird identification differ from how the practice of "field ornithology," or birding, as it is conducted today? First and foremost, identifications were made in the hand, not in the field, using traits that could be noted in the hand. Bird identification today is focused on traits that can be noted at a distance, in the field, using optics. And while field identification has come a long way in the hundred years since binoculars and spotting scopes replaced the shotgun, a trio of tenets of this older approach to bird identification lingered.

First, and for many years, bird-watchers continued to rely heavily upon structural- and plumage-related traits to distinguish one species from the next. Many of these traits are subtle and difficult to see at a distance. In other words, bird identification continued to rely on noting details.

Second, a focus on behavioral characteristics lagged. Bird specimens in a drawer behave more or less alike. In life, birds forage and fly and behave in ways that are characteristic of their species.

Third, the identification process continued to focus on birds as isolated and disjunct elements—separated from the environments that supported them. Like specimens in a drawer, birds were, in essence, taken out of context, out of their supporting habitat.

That is precisely where the art of field identification begins.

2 | Point of Departure

I n 1934, a twenty-four-year-old "student of birds" wrote and illustrated a book that was the prototype for all the field guides that followed. His name was Roger Tory Peterson. His book, entitled *A Field Guide to the Birds,* ushered in the avocation of bird watching.

In that book's brief, five-page introduction is the core of the book you now hold in your hands. One part of that discussion, consuming the better part of a page, stands out. It is subtitled "Identification by Elimination." It counsels that the way to approach the identification process is to start by reducing the number of variables. Happily, and to a large degree, birds have already done much of that work for you. All you need to do is recognize this and benefit from it.

In an earlier book, *The Art of Bird Finding,* I recounted my early frustration trying to find some much-sought-after birds. According to the range maps in the very simplified field guide I was using, the birds I sought should have been found in North Jersey, where I started birding. But I couldn't find them.

Wood Thrush, Scarlet Tanager, Rufous-sided (now Eastern) Towhee and lots of other cool birds were easy to locate in the woodland behind my parent's suburban home. But other species, most notably Horned Lark, Eastern Meadowlark, and Vesper Sparrow, proved very elusive. There was a reason for this.

The birds I had trouble finding were grassland species, specialized to be in open habitat dominated by grasses. The habitat behind

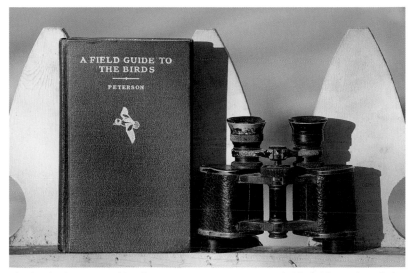

The book that started it all: Roger Tory Peterson's A Field Guide to the Birds, *published in 1934, shown here with a LeMaire binocular similar to the one the 24-year-old "student of birds" used during his early years.*

our house was deciduous woodland, habitat wholly unsuited for grassland bird species.

Beginning birders tend to approach their new interest existentially: Every new encounter with a bird is unique and disjunct. They focus wholly on the bird, commonly ignoring the cause-and-effect relationships that prompt a bird to be *here*, not *there*, and here *now*, not *some other time*. Just as with specimens in a drawer, they take the bird out of context.

What a bird is is directly related to the morphological traits that distinguish it. What these traits do is give birds an adaptive advantage in certain habitats—and it is in these habitats that the bird is going to be found.

Take this wisdom to the bank: Birds are almost always where they are supposed to be.

As a beginning birder, you can bring little experience to bear when it comes to recognizing the birds you encounter. But you can certainly recognize basic habitats. You can tell grassland from forest, desert from mangrove swamp, freshwater marsh from tidal estuary.

Birds are almost always where they are supposed to be, which explains why I never could find this grassland-loving Vesper Sparrow in the woods behind my parents' house.

Different birds are specialized to live in these different habitats. So your very first step in the identification process begins with something your experience can readily bring to bear. It starts with recognizing the habitat around you and understanding that bird species are *bound to* and *found in* specific habitats.

Think of habitat as a theater or arena or stadium—a place where you and birds will interact. If you go to a concert theater, you can expect to find musicians. If you go to a rodeo arena, be prepared to see calf ropers and bull riders. Go to a football stadium and . . .

You get the idea.

So if you go to the Metropolitan Opera, you are going to find tenors and baritones, not tight ends and linebackers. If you go to Olympia National Forest, you are going to find Steller's Jays and Band-tailed Pigeons, not Limpkins and Purple Gallinules (for these you can try the Everglades).

Following is a list and descriptions of the basic habitats and principal species or bird groups that are found there. Your first task, as a new birder, is to recognize and appreciate the link between bird groups and their habitats—especially the habitats near you.

Major North American Habitats and the Bird Groups They Support

Arctic Tundra. A terrestrial habitat found in arctic regions, where cold temperatures and a short growing season support only stunted, ground-hugging plants. In summer: raptors, ptarmigan, shorebirds, ravens, wagtails and pipits, sparrows, finches. Lakes and rivers support loons, waterfowl, gulls and terns. In winter: precious little.

Alpine Tundra. A stunted tundra habitat found at high altitudes (in North America, primarily in the western mountains). In summer: raptors, swifts, ravens, Clark's Nutcracker, Horned Lark, swallows, wrens, American Pipit, sparrows, rosy-finches.

Taiga (Boreal Forest). A northern forest type dominated by conifers (primarily spruce) that stretches from Alaska to eastern Canada and defines the southern boundary of the arctic tundra. In summer: raptors, owls, woodpeckers, flycatchers, crows and jays, swallows, chickadees, kinglets, thrushes, wood-warblers, sparrows, blackbirds, finches, and other species. Lakes and rivers support loons, grebes, waterfowl, rails, cranes, shorebirds, gulls and terns. In winter: some hawks and owls, grouse, crows and jays, chickadees, finches.

Desert. An arid habitat characterized by sparse, usually short, often spiny plants; some grasses; bare earth; and, in summer, high temperatures. Raptors, quail, pigeons and doves, Greater Roadrunner, owls, goatsuckers, hummingbirds, woodpeckers, flycatchers, ravens, swallows, Verdin, wrens, gnatcatchers, thrashers, sparrows, orioles, finches. Many of these species are year-round residents.

Savanna. Expansive grassland dotted with trees or small stands of trees. Vultures, raptors, game birds, pigeons and doves, owls, woodpeckers, flycatchers, crows and jays, swallows, chickadees and titmice, wrens, bluebirds, sparrows, orioles, finches.

Grassland/Prairie. Habitat dominated by grasses and forbs and devoid of trees. Vultures, raptors, game birds, some shorebirds,

Grassland vs. forest and alpine tundra. If you can distinguish between these habitats, you are well on your way toward simplifying the bird identification challenge.

pigeons and doves, Greater Roadrunner, goatsuckers, flycatchers, ravens and magpies, Horned Lark, swallows, wrens, pipits, sparrows, blackbirds, finches. Note: Grassland is bisected by riparian (tree-lined) corridors and bodies of water. Expect additional species where prairie abuts different habitat.

Chaparral. Coastal scrub (in the United States, limited to coastal California) consisting of short, spiny evergreen shrubs. Vultures, raptors, flycatchers, Wrentit, California Thrasher, sparrows.

Temperate Forest. A widespread and varied habitat dominated by tall coniferous and/or deciduous trees that may or may not support an understory. Raptors, game birds, cuckoos, owls, goatsuckers, hummingbirds, woodpeckers, flycatchers, vireos, crows and jays, chickadees and titmice, wrens, kinglets, gnatcatchers, thrushes, wood-warblers, tanagers, sparrows, blackbirds, finches.

Tropical Deciduous Forest. A habitat dominated by tall deciduous evergreens with a closed canopy and replete with vines and epiphytes (in North America, limited to southern Florida). Herons, vultures, raptors, pigeons and doves, cuckoos, owls, goatsuckers, woodpeckers, flycatchers, vireos, jays, gnatcatchers, wood-warblers, and other woodland species.

Lakes/Ponds/Rivers. Aquatic habitat that can be bounded by a variety of other habitat types. Loons, grebes, pelicans, cormorants, herons, waterfowl, gulls and terns, kingfishers. Exposed shorelines often support shorebirds, corvids, and other species. Swifts, swallows, flycatchers, and some other species commonly hunt for insects over water surfaces.

Freshwater Marsh. An aquatic habitat supporting lush cattails, bullrush, sedges, and rank weeds. Grebes, herons, waterfowl, rails, cranes, gulls and terns, wrens, sparrows, blackbirds.

Tidal or Salt Marsh. A coastal aquatic habitat dominated by salt-tolerant grasses (primarily *Spartina*). Tidal creeks, rivers, salt-marsh ponds, and mudflats that are exposed on a falling tide also add character to this habitat. Grebes, cormorants, herons, waterfowl, raptors, rails, shorebirds, gulls and terns, owls, swallows, sparrows, blackbirds.

Pelagic. Open ocean: in North America, the Atlantic and Pacific plus the Gulf of Mexico and Beaufort Sea. Loons, grebes, albatrosses, shearwaters, petrels and storm-petrels, boobies and

Freshwater marsh supports birds specialized to forage in wet places, including the Limpkin, a large rail whose diet consists largely of apple snails.

gannets, pelicans, cormorants, waterfowl, phalaropes, gulls and terns, alcids.

Sandy and Rocky Coastline. The usually narrow band of habitat lying between ocean and upland, defined largely by scant vegetation or none. Pelicans, cormorants, herons, waterfowl, shorebirds, gulls and terns, larks, swallows, crows, blackbirds, raptors, House Finch, Snow Bunting.

Urban Areas. A habitat type dominated by tall, man-made structures but dotted with islands of vegetated habitat (parks). Raptors, gulls, pigeons, parrots (mostly in Florida, Texas, and California), swifts, crows, swallows, starlings, sparrows, blackbirds, finches. In migration, many species are possible in vegetative oases.

Suburbia. A patchwork habitat characterized by a mix of natural and highly managed, nonnative vegetation and man-made structures, including roads and parking lots. Raptors, game birds, gulls, pigeons and doves, owls, swifts, hummingbirds, woodpeckers, flycatchers, vireos, crows and jays, swallows, chickadees and titmice, robins, mimids, European Starling, sparrows, blackbirds, finches.

Agricultural Land. A managed habitat that supports a monotypic, nonnative plant that is periodically partially or totally removed, leaving denuded, sometimes bare, turned earth. Herons, vultures, waterfowl, raptors, game birds, rails, cranes, shorebirds, gulls, pigeons and doves, owls, flycatchers, crows, larks, swallows, robins, European Starling, pipits, some warblers, sparrows, blackbirds, finches.

Over time, your sense of habitat will grow more discriminating. You will learn and appreciate, for instance, the difference between forests dominated by conifers, forests dominated by deciduous trees, and forests that have a mix of both. Where I live, in southern New Jersey, Scarlet Tanagers occur in mature deciduous woodland while the closely related Summer Tanager occurs in mature mixed woodland characterized by oaks and pines.

Some species are less picky than others and able to occupy a variety of habitats. Downy Woodpeckers are found in forest interiors, suburban landscapes, weedy lots in urban areas, and cattail marshes, where they search for insect larvae on the stalks of rank weeds. The larger Hairy Woodpecker is a bird of mature woodland and forests. I have been birding for more than fifty years and I have seen many Hairy Woodpeckers. But I have never seen one on a cattail stalk.

Other species are even more specific in their habitat requirements. The road I walk every morning bisects two types of marsh: tidal marsh dominated by *Spartina* grass on one side, freshwater marsh dominated by Phragmites and cattail on the other. In the tidal marsh, Seaside Sparrows abound. But I have rarely seen an adult Seaside Sparrow cross the road into the freshwater marsh. Breeding in the freshwater marsh is Swamp Sparrow (in fact, a rare subspecies). Almost never does the Swamp Sparrow cross over to the tidal side.

Why would they move? They are different species bound to and divided by their habitat requirements.

A species' range you will check later. Temporal distribution and relative abundance, too. For beginning birders, these qualifying considerations come at the *end* of the identification process and are a litmus test of your initial identification.

But the link between what a bird is specialized for and the habitat it frequents is only slightly less immutable than what it is and how it appears.

And look what's happened! You have greatly simplified the identification process—just like Roger Tory Peterson counseled. By understanding the link between birds and habitat, you have eliminated scores, even hundreds, of possibilities because you are in habitat X and many species will not be found there.

Even before you raise your binoculars, even before you see a bird, habitat has already simplified the identification process for you.

Turkey Point, New Jersey, has breeding Seaside Sparrows and Swamp Sparrows. Swamp Sparrows stay in the freshwater marshes; Seaside Sparrows (shown here) stick to the tidal saltwater side.

3 | So You Want to Identify a Bird. Take a Seat.

For new birders, flipping through the pages of a field guide can be sobering. So many species. So many unfamiliar names. So many species (and names!) that are more alike than not.

You may not appreciate it yet, but this shared similarity actually works to your advantage. Instead of being overwhelmed, try approaching the challenge of bird identification from a positive footing. Case in point: Have you ever calculated the number of birds you can recognize right now because they are common and distinctive and you've seen them before? Birds like duck, goose, heron, hawk, sandpiper, gull, crow, pigeon, and turkey? Maybe jay, woodpecker, hummingbird, robin, sparrow, blackbird, and chickadee?

Very likely there are other birds you can name at a glance. If you live in coastal Florida or California, you are probably familiar with pelicans. If you are a hunter, you probably recognize pheasant, grouse, or quail. Anyone who has spent any time in the country knows swallows, and you don't have to live in St. Louis to recognize a cardinal (hint: it's the red bird commonly perched on a holly branch that festoons half the holiday cards you receive).

And you are thinking, "Big deal. So I know a handful of birds. What I'm interested in is learning how to identify the birds I *don't* know."

Patience. In bird identification, as in life, when you confront a new challenge, you begin by bringing your experience to bear. From this footing, you then step into the unknown. The identification process used by the most experienced birders in the world works the same way—by first bringing their compounded wisdom to bear, measuring and comparing every new identification challenge with species they are already familiar with. You, as a beginner, differ from experts only by degrees; in fact, you probably have no idea how advanced you already are. Your current skill level has already moved you into the next phase of the bird identification challenge.

You are already familiar with, and have a foundation in, the breaking up of birds into different subgroups—birds that are grouped together because of their common traits. Without getting into particulars, the birds just named are representatives of bird subgroups, scientific orders or families—birds whose shared traits bind them into a group and distinguish them from other groups.

After recognizing habitat, getting birds into the right subgroup is the next step in the identification process. If habitat is like a stadium or concert hall, placing birds in the right order is akin to getting to the right seating section. Bird families can be thought of as a row of seats. Individual species— the identification endgame—are akin to the seats in a row.

So identifying a bird is like finding an assigned seat. You start by going to the stadium, then locating the seating section, then your row, then your seat. Or, translated into birdspeak, first you go to the proper habitat.

Example: northern forest, home to certain hawks, owls, woodpeckers, flycatchers, thrushes, warblers, finches, and other bird families specialized for primarily coniferous woodland. Once you find a bird, you note the manifest characteristics that place it in a specific bird group, its order, then its family: traits such as the size and shape of the bird, the shape of the bill, the length of its legs . . .

From here on in, pinning the name to a bird is just a matter of details. These you will find in your field guide.

"But I don't want any of this sort-and-package mumbo jumbo. I just want to identify this freaking bird!"

There are probably a few readers who are thinking right about now that this is a really tedious approach to bird identification. All you really want to do is just go outside with your new binoculars and field guide or identification app, find a bird, and then match it with its picture.

Well . . . go ahead. But mark this page. And come back when you get frustrated.

Let me tell you what is going to happen. You are going to go out. Find a bird. One crouched on your lawn, let's say. You note what you assume are important traits: size of a robin (but definitely not a robin), mostly brownish overall with lots of spots on the underparts, and a really pointy bill.

You open your guide. Start flipping through the pages. Stop at the first plate showing a whole bunch of brown-backed, spot-breasted birds.

"Ha! Thrushes. That wasn't so hard."

You pick one that seems most like the bird you saw—the one with the most prominent black spots. But . . .

"Hmmm. Bird didn't seem quite that brown above."

So you start flipping back through the guide and get to . . .

"Ah, thrashers! That's what it was. . . . Except I think the bill was straighter."

And then you discover that there's another group of birds called wrens and one of them is all brown above with black spots, too. And you haven't even hit the sparrows yet.

Having fun?

The bird, by the way, was a female Northern Flicker. A woodpecker. From a family characterized by chisel-shaped bills, long bodies, short, scraggly tails, and very short legs (not to mention feet that have two toes forward and two toes aft—a trait difficult to see in the field). A family that, anatomically speaking, is about as close to thrushes as orchestra pit seating is to the second tier.

Where you went wrong was not putting the bird in the right family group right at the start *and* not giving due regard to habitat.

The spot-breasted thrushes are, for the most part, woodland species. Thrashers and wrens are more likely to be in brush than on lawns.

But a woodpecker? On the ground? Yep. Some woodpecker species, including Acorn, Red-headed, and Pileated, commonly light on the ground (or on fallen branches) when feeding (other woodpecker species sally forth and snap insects out of the air, and several species pluck berries off vines).

Incidentally, it might interest you to know that the flicker you found was the very first bird that Roger Tory Peterson identified—the bird that propelled him to a life of bird study. It was on the ground, too, resting at the base of a tree.

Back to Finding the Seating Section

You probably noted something as you flipped through your field guide, searching for that spot-breasted bird. Right. The birds are grouped. Did you note how they were grouped? Order and family. Right again.

As we were discussing, this is where your current skill level and the identification process cross. You've already got a sense of what some of the common bird family groups are: ducks, hawks, gulls, jays, sparrows . . . and now woodpeckers. You can distinguish them because, as a group, they have very obvious characteristics—relating mostly to size, shape, and overall plumage—that distinguish them from other groups.

So build on this. Give yourself a better sense of what this bird-grouping stuff is all about so the next time you find an unfamiliar species, your basic skill set will be up to the challenge.

Even though you can already recognize many family groups, you are not yet playing with a full deck. There are more bird groups than you are aware of. Not all are quite so obvious as the difference between, say, ducks and hawks, or thrushes and woodpeckers.

There are more than seventy family groups in North America. Some are very large, meaning they include a number of different species that are widely represented across North America. Some are small, even limited to a single species.

In most field guides, family groups appear in a specific sequence based on their evolutionary refinements. More "primitive" birds are presented first. Birds more evolutionarily advanced follow.

Open your guide and look at them. No—not the individual species! Just the groupings. Read about the traits and behavioral characteristics that both unite them and distinguish them from other bird families.

That's right. It's not just time to familiarize yourself with the major bird groupings, it is time to familiarize yourself with your field guide. The two of you are going to be a birding team for a long time. The book you are holding now is just a dating service.

Here's a bit of good news. The family groups you are probably already familiar with constitute the bulk of North America's eight hundred or so regularly occurring bird species. If you can recognize herons, ducks, geese, hawks, sandpipers, gulls and terns, pigeons and doves, hummingbirds, woodpeckers, jays and crows, chickadees, thrushes, sparrows, and blackbirds, you are on familiar terms with more than half of North America's birds.

You know their family; identifying species is now just a matter of getting acquainted with the family members.

There are really only five large family groups that you probably have little or no familiarity with: the shearwaters and petrels (family Procellariidae); the auks, murres, and puffins (family Alcidae); tyrant flycatchers (family Tyrannidae); the wood-warblers (family Parulidae); and the finches (family Fringillidae). Two of these families are found almost wholly in marine environments, so unless the Atlantic or Pacific Ocean constitute your backyard, you can simplify your studies and leave the Procellariidae and Alcidae for later.

Wait a minute, you're thinking, I cheated. Two paragraphs back, I gave you credit for being thrush conversant.

Yes, I did. You know American Robin, and a robin is a thrush. If you know robin—know how it's shaped, how it stands, how it walks (or does it hop?), how it feeds—then you are familiar with one member of the family that can introduce you to the other North American thrushes: Bluethroat, Northern Wheatear, Eastern Bluebird, Western Bluebird, Mountain Bluebird, Townsend's Solitaire,

American Robin. Your neighborhood thrush. If you know robins—how they stand, fly, forage—then you know a great deal about other members of the thrush family.

Veery, Gray-cheeked Thrush, Bicknell's Thrush, Swainson's Thrush, Hermit Thrush, Wood Thrush, Clay-colored Robin, and Varied Thrush.

Maybe you're feeling a little sheepish now, thinking, "well, when I admitted to knowing a robin I didn't say I was intimate with it. Don't know how it stands and walks . . . or does it hop?"

I know. It's time you learned. This goes for herons, ducks, geese, hawks, sandpipers, gulls, pigeons, hummingbirds, woodpeckers, jays, crows, chickadees, sparrows, blackbirds, and all the other birds you can already recognize. These are your bellwether birds, the ones whose familiarity will lead you to their next of kin.

Kenn Kaufman is fond of noting that the way to recognize uncommon species is to gain familiarity with the common ones first. That goes for your fundamental understanding of family groups, too. Learn the characteristics that link members of a bird family together before looking for the details that make each species distinct.

You have two assignments:

1. Familiarize yourself with your field guide. Recognize the order and arrangement of bird groups. Become familiar with and recognize the traits that bind family groups together.
2. Go out and study the common birds that you already recognize, your local representatives of family groups. Learn how they stand, move, forage, fly. Become intimate with them. (There's a name for this activity. It's called "bird watching.")

By the way, American Robins both walk and hop. Most thrushes just hop.

I won't make you fend for yourself. Following are descriptions of the characteristics of all the major North American bird groups as well as common representatives of each group. There will be a test later.

 WATERFOWL (*Anseriformes*): Ducks, Geese, Swans

A very large and mostly colorful (males, at least) order made up of largely aquatic birds characterized by blunt, flattened (i.e., "duck") bills, long necks, plump bodies, short tails, short and sturdy legs, and webbed feet. They range in size from the ten-inch Bufflehead to the sixty-inch Trumpeter Swan. Some of the ducks are known as dabblers, birds that upend and reach down to pluck food from the bottom; some dive for food. Many of the dabblers, all geese, and all swans can and do forage on dry, often agricultural, land, and a few (such as Wood Duck and the whistling-ducks) perch in trees. Nests are sometimes far from water.

These birds are highly social, often found in flocks, and commonly vocal. Vocalizations are not limited to quacks and honks.

Waterfowl include ducks, geese, and swans. They vary in size and plumage, but all have "ducklike" bills, including (and perhaps most notably) the Northern Shoveler, whose outsized bill is the source of its name. Pictured here are the colorful male and cryptic female.

Some species whistle, squeal, grunt, cackle, croak, coo . . . and some are all but mute. Many species pair in fall or early winter, aiding in the identification of the usually more cryptic females (which will be close by the male).

Birds commonly mistaken for waterfowl include loons, grebes, coots, cormorants.

Your local representatives from this group are Mallard, Canada Goose, and any swan.

GAME BIRDS (*Galliformes*): Quail, Pheasants, Grouse

Medium to large mostly ground-dwelling birds of dry, upland terrain characterized by very short, pointy (somewhat conical) bills; short, thick necks; plump bodies; and fairly short, sturdy legs. Except for pheasants, sage-grouse, and Sharp-tailed Grouse, birds in this group show short, blunt tails.

Most birds in this group are basically brown or gray; some (mostly males) are colorfully patterned. Game birds tend to be shy and very adept at hiding in vegetation, and commonly walk (or run) when approached. When flushed, they explode into flight, propelling themselves with rapid wing beats; when landing, they commonly set their wings and glide.

Many species are social, and vocal, particularly after birds are flushed and flocks reform.

Your local representatives from this group include whatever grouse or quail lives near you, Ring-necked Pheasant, and Wild Turkey.

 LOONS (*Gaviidae*)

Large swimming and diving birds with daggerlike bills; short, thick necks; long bodies that sit low to the water; and no apparent tails. Except during the breeding season, birds are brownish gray right to the waterline. Throats and breasts (and underparts) are white.

Found in open water on large freshwater lakes, bays, and oceans (often many miles from shore). Except in migration, mostly solitary or found in pairs. Feed by diving and often remain underwater for thirty seconds or more. Unless sick or injured (or incubating) almost never seen on land. Takeoffs are labored, with birds running across the water surface. In flight, wing beats are rubbery and constant. The feet trail behind the bird, suggesting a tail. Except during the breeding season, expect birds to be silent. May be confused with some grebes and, particularly, cormorants.

You may not have a local representative for this group, but loons can often be seen in coastal waters and on large inland lakes in April and May, particularly after a cold front or storm passes.

 GREBES (*Podicipedidae*)

Like small loons but slender necked and shorter billed and more squared-off in the rear, often showing a short, up-cocked nub of a tail. Exceptions to this generalization are Red-necked Grebes, whose size, bill, and shape are very loonlike, and Clark's and Western Grebes, whose bills are rapier-thin (not daggerlike) and necks are sinuously long (not at all loonlike). Grebes swim like loons, dive like loons, and, like loons, are almost never seen out of water.

Generally more social than loons (particularly Eared Grebes, which in winter gather in flocks numbering in the hundreds). Commonly swim or dive from danger, fly reluctantly, and, like loons, need a running takeoff. Surfacing birds may remain mostly submerged, and grebes are much more likely to be found amid floating vegetation than are loons.

Pied-billed Grebe is the most widespread, but in winter, in parts of the West, Eared Grebe can be abundant on inland lakes.

 TUBE-NOSES (*Procellariiformes*): Albatrosses, Shearwaters, Petrels, Fulmars, Storm-Petrels

Pelagic (ocean-dwelling) birds uncommonly seen near land (or from the shore) and much less commonly found on inland bodies of water. Inland encounters are mostly storm, often hurricane, related. Except for storm-petrels, which are small and somewhat swallow-like, these pelagic birds most closely resemble large, long-winged gulls. Most are grayish above and white below (some are dark bodied), and most glide for extended periods just above the surface of the water on long, stiff wings (storm-petrels flutter and often tack or zig-zag just above the surface).

Many species sit in large "rafts" on the water, particularly in calm seas. Often found near feeding whales. May be confused with gulls and jaegers. Albatrosses, owing to their size, can be confused only with Northern Gannet.

PELICANS AND ALLIES (*Pelecaniformes*): Tropicbirds, Frigatebirds, Boobies, Gannets, Cormorants, Anhingas

A diverse, mostly aquatic, and mostly ocean-based assemblage. Among this group, only the cormorants, Anhinga, and pelicans are likely to be seen away from coastal areas. All eat fish (or squid). All have webbed feet. Some swim and dive, some plunge from the air, some snatch food from the ocean surface or pirate food.

Except for cormorants, which may easily be confused with loons (or Anhinga), and tropicbirds, which might be mistaken for large terns, the families in this order are very distinctive.

FLAMINGOES (*Phoenicopteridae*)

Distinctive and unique. The only place in North America to see a Greater Flamingo is extreme southern Florida, where some wild birds hailing from the Bahamas may be found. Other flamingoes seen in the wild are escapees from zoos.

HERONS AND ALLIES (*Ciconiiformes*):
Herons, Ibis, Spoonbills, Storks

A group of mostly large to very large, long-necked, long-legged wading birds. Most feed by standing in, or stalking across, open shallow water. Most have long, pointy bills used to spear prey. Many have shaggy crests or showy plumes (in the breeding season). A goodly number (but certainly not all) are entirely or mostly white.

Exceptions to these generalizations include ibis, which have down-curved bills, and Roseate Spoonbill, whose long, straight bill has a widened, spoonlike tip. Also, Cattle Egret is rarely seen standing in water, and Great Blue Heron, Great Egret, Black-crowned Night-Heron, and ibis sometimes forage on dry ground (pastures, lawns, rocky shorelines).

The smaller Green Heron often hunts from a perch within stabbing distance of water. Bitterns forage along the edge, in aquatic reeds and marshes, not commonly in open water. Note: The butterscotch-colored Least Bittern is tiny, smaller than a pigeon. American Bittern is as large as, and shaped much like, the night-herons.

Yet and still, most of the birds in this group are large, distinctive, and not particularly shy. One bird commonly mistaken for a heron, and vice versa, is the Sandhill Crane. While cranes commonly roost in open water, they forage on dry land or marsh and have tails that look like wilted feather dusters. Herons appear tailless.

 VULTURES (*Cathartidae*) AND BIRDS OF PREY
(*Falconiformes*): Hawks, Falcons, Kites, Eagles

A large bird group made larger by the inclusion of the vultures. Hawks, eagles, falcons, and kites have hooked bills for tearing and taloned feet for grasping prey. While otherwise akin to those of the "diurnal birds of prey," vultures have feet that are not suited for grasping. Also, the heads of vultures are unfeathered. Birds of prey have feathered heads.

Birds of prey range in size from the robin-sized American Kestrel to the very large Bald and Golden Eagles. Most are birds of open country or forest edge. They are commonly seen perched, often on exposed branches or telephone poles, or soaring overhead.

Most are dark (commonly brown) above and paler and patterned below, although many, particularly western, species may be entirely or mostly dark bodied. They are generally shy and fly away when approached. Mostly solitary or seen as pairs, but in migration, a few species gather in large flocks.

Other birds habitually harass, or "mob," perched or flying raptors or take flight when raptors approach. In flight, raptors commonly soar on set wings, circling to gain altitude. But this is not unique to birds of prey: Storks, cranes, gulls, and other species groups soar as well. Birds most commonly confused with birds of prey include gulls, crows, and ravens.

A local representative is the widespread Red-tailed Hawk, which often perches along roadsides.

 RAILS AND ALLIES (Gruiformes): Coots, Gallinules, Cranes

A group of mostly shy, mostly marshland birds that are more commonly heard than seen. Ranging in size from the sparrow-sized Black Rail to the heron-sized Whooping Crane, most members of this group are pigeon-sized or smaller and behave somewhat like nervous chickens, walking (or swimming) slowly with jerky movements.

Excepting cranes, whose bills are heronlike, the bills of rails are stubby and chickenlike or long, pointy, and downward drooping. Their bodies are somewhat vase shaped (smaller species, such as Black Sora and Yellow Rail, appear neckless). Tails are mostly short and up-cocked. Legs are long and sturdy; feet are large with long toes.

Rails are commonly seen only in glimpses (if at all) as they skulk through the vegetative edge of some body of water. They swim well but reluctantly. Purple Gallinules swim but commonly stay close to vegetation, often climbing and clambering among emergent vegetation and bushes. American Coots habitually swim in the open and, along with gallinules, sometimes forage on land (they are very partial to lawns).

Excepting cranes and Limpkin, all members of this group are loath to flush, and fly with effort and commonly not far (coots rarely even get airborne; they just run across the water).

Sandhill Cranes are heronlike, large, and more terrestrial; the very rare Whooping Crane is larger than any heron but, like herons, mostly aquatic, foraging in wetlands or shallow, open water. Cranes fly with necks outstretched (as do all members of this group), unlike herons, which commonly draw their necks in.

The smaller rails may be confused with shorebirds. Coots and gallinules may be mistaken for small ducks; cranes and Limpkin, for herons.

 SHOREBIRDS: Plovers (*Charadriidae*), Sandpipers (*Scolopacidae*)

As the name implies, a large group of birds that mostly favor open habitats where earth and water meet—beaches, shorelines, mudflats, shallow ponds—but many species favor open, dry uplands, including plowed fields, short grass, and rocky coasts, and a few favor open ocean. Plovers, with short, somewhat blunt bills, generally favor higher, drier habitats; pointier-billed sandpipers generally like to keep their feet (sometimes their entire legs and heads) wet.

Some species, such as Least Sandpiper, are tiny, smaller than a sparrow. Some, such as Long-billed Curlew and Marbled Godwit, are the size of ducks. Most are robin-sized or smaller. While some species are very distinctive, even flamboyant, most members of this group are less distinctly patterned. In spring and early summer, many do wear a more eye-catching breeding plumage, but juvenile birds and nonbreeding adults are overall pretty bland—grayish or brownish above, pale below.

Sandpipers are very active, sometimes frenetic, feeders—stitching, probing, and stabbing as they wade or walk. Plovers are more deliberate: walk, stop, pick (like robins). Most shorebirds are highly social, often found in large flocks. Habitat choice and feeding behavior help when it comes to determining species. Also, in winter and migration, these birds commonly gather in mixed-species flocks, facilitating comparison. Very vocal, often calling when flushed or when flying overhead, and many calls are distinctive.

Sandpipers may be mistaken for rails, but rails are far more likely to be close to, if not in, vegetation. Plovers might be mistaken only for sandpipers.

GULLS, TERNS, AND ALLIES (*Laridae*)

A large and widespread group that is easily distinguished from other groups but often difficult to separate from each other. Many species have similar plumages, and many go through several plumage changes as they mature.

They are most commonly found near large, open bodies of water. Many gull species also frequent agricultural land, shopping malls, and open landfills. Some terns (and some gulls) breed and hunt in freshwater and saltwater marshes.

Gulls are mostly overall robust, large headed, thick necked, big chested, and long winged, and stand with a horizontal profile. Bills are short and straight, often with a hooked tip. Tails short and blunt. Legs short, sturdy, bare, and set about mid-span between the tip of the bill and the tail.

Terns are overall more slender and generally smaller than gulls. Pointier billed, shorter necked, with shorter legs and a longer body profile. Tails are long to very long and notched to deeply forked. Jaegers, which breed in the arctic and spend the balance of their lives at sea, are as robust as gulls but as nimble at terns.

Gulls and terns are highly social, breeding in colonies, feeding in large flocks, and "loafing" in tightly packed groups. Gulls sit on

While many gull species are difficult to identify, Laughing Gulls in breeding plumage side toward the easy end of the scale.

the water, walk (with an ambling sailor's gait) easily and well, hover with effort, and drop or plop to the water's surface. Terns rarely sit on the water, shuffle short distances, hover nimbly, and dive headfirst into the water or deftly snatch food from the surface without landing.

On the East Coast, Herring Gull and the smaller Ring-billed Gull are the two most common gulls. On the West Coast, Western Gull is the default gull.

 ALCIDS (*Alcidae*): Auks, Murres, Puffins

A group of pelagic birds, uncommonly seen from shore, that resemble tiny penguins—particularly when standing on land, which, except during the breeding season, they rarely do. The puffin is probably the member of this group familiar to most people. Overall stocky and thick necked, with bodies shaped like footballs, most species are black above, white below. Most have short, pointy bills, but the bills of murres are loonlike, and puffins' are bulbously swollen.

Alcids spend much of the day floating on the ocean surface and diving for prey, often in small flocks. They are strong fliers, flying just above the water surface with wing beats so fast they blur.

PIGEONS AND DOVES (*Columbidae*)

Small to medium-sized birds of fields, farmlands, and forests, with plump bodies, short, sturdy legs, and small heads with tiny bills that thicken near the tip. Pigeons are robust and overall darker bodied; doves are smaller, paler (many brownish or grayish), often with longer and narrower tails.

Doves, feeding chiefly on grain and seeds, forage on the ground (as does the introduced and widespread Rock Pigeon). Movements are somewhat jerky and often wandering. Native North American pigeons commonly forage in trees, often in small flocks, and are often seen perched on bare branches just above the canopy. The common and widespread Mourning Dove habitually perches on utility lines. Generally tame, birds in this group will allow a close approach before exploding into flight. They are very vocal; the calls of whatever species is near you are a big part of the audio landscape.

Everyone is familiar with the Rock Pigeon. Mourning Dove in the East and White-winged Dove in the West and the increasingly widespread Collared Dove are representatives to study.

PARROTS AND PARAKEETS (*Psittacidae*)

A large, noisy, colorful (mostly green), and familiar group of tropical birds characterized by powerful "parrotlike" bills. Established populations of many different nonnative species occur primarily in Florida, Texas, and California. The Monk Parakeet, a native of South America, is more widespread.

CUCKOOS (*Cuculidae*)

A group of slender, long-tailed, and generally surreptitious birds that maneuver through the foliage. Mostly brown above and creamy white below with a boldly patterned undertail. Often only the head and short, claw-shaped bill is visible. Spend long periods without moving. Movements are sluggish, deliberate. When flushed, fly strongly and directly, disappearing into the foliage. Perch with an upright posture, but occasionally lean forward as if about to fly.

An exception is the Greater Roadrunner of the Southwest, a large, shaggy-crested, long-tailed, and mostly ground-foraging cuckoo that flies much less frequently than it walks or runs.

Cuckoos may be mistaken for thrashers, but thrashers like to sit high, out in the open. Cuckoos commonly do not.

OWLS (*Strigiformes*)

A celebrated, mostly nocturnal group of predatory birds that are widespread and commonly heard but difficult to see. They range in size from the sparrow-sized Elf Owl of the Southwest to the large Great Gray Owl of the boreal forest and occupy an array of habitats—from the arctic ice cap to forest interiors, grassland, desert scrub, and suburban woodlots.

For the most part, owls appear stocky and neckless, with large heads and front-set eyes framed by facial disks. Grays and browns are the dominant colors, with some birds showing touches of orange or rust. Legs and feet are feathered (unlike most hawks'), and some species sport short ear tufts, which may or may not be visible.

Usually solitary, some species (most notably Long-eared and Short-eared Owls) may roost communally. In daylight, roosting owls are frequently harassed by chickadees, titmice, jays, and

While owls may be challenging to locate, they are not necessarily uncommon. The Great Horned Owl is one of the most widespread species in North America. This pair was roosting in a riparian woodland in the Comanche National Grassland of southeast Colorado.

crows, and attentive observers can be alerted to their location. While mostly nocturnal, some species do hunt during the day. These include Snowy Owl, Northern Hawk Owl, Short-eared Owl, Ferruginous and Northern Pygmy-Owl, and Barred Owl.

Owls are quite distinctive. Turning a perched hawk into an owl is usually accomplished only with a lavish amount of wishful thinking.

GOATSUCKERS (*Caprimulgidae*): Nighthawks, Nightjars (Whip-poor-wills, et al.)

A group of nocturnal or crepuscular birds characterized by tiny bills but *big* mouths and very cryptic plumage. Sitting out the day, as they do, astride a tree limb or on the leafy forest floor, their eye-defeating gray or brown plumage serves them well.

Ranging from the starling-sized Common Poorwill of the West to the long-tailed Common Pauraque, whose range extends into southeastern Texas, the birds are best known for their calls, which are, for many species, the source of their names: poorwill, Chuck-will's-widow, Whip-poor-will, pauraque.

Pointy-winged nighthawks can often be seen wheeling batlike in twilight skies or over well-lit urban areas and bodies of water. Other members of this group are blunter winged, hunt from the ground or from perches, and sally out (or up) to snag insect prey (primarily large moths).

SWIFTS (*Apodidae*)

In the immortal words of Roger Tory Peterson, "a cigar butt with wings." Swifts combine short, mostly stubby bodies with long, slender, scimitarlike wings.

North American swifts are overall dark brown or blackish (the well-marked White-throated Swift excepted). Almost never seen perched, the birds spend most of their time aloft, foraging for insects, often at very high altitudes but also particularly after rains, just above the surface of lakes. Flight is as the name suggests: swift. Wing beats are rapid and quivering. Glides may be prolonged and often appear unsteady or wobbly. Birds commonly forage in flocks (sometimes with swallows), with the swifts sweeping past the others with superior speed and finesse.

The wings of swallows are wider and angled back; those of swifts more slender and curved. Also, swallows are generally more colorful and patterned than are most swifts. Only the black-and-white, fork-tailed White-throated Swift might be mistaken for a swallow.

 TROGONS (*Trogonidae*)

A family of large, large-headed, long-tailed, tubular-shaped birds of tropical and subtropical regions. Colorful and sluggish. Only one species, the Elegant Trogon, regularly occurs north of Mexico; its range is limited to southeastern Arizona and southwestern New Mexico.

 HUMMINGBIRDS (*Trochilidae*)

Tiny jewels on wings. You might mistake these mostly nectar-feeding birds for large insects, but you will not confuse them with any other group of birds. The insects most commonly mistaken for hummingbirds are the hummingbird moths, which, like hummingbirds, hover in front of flowers on wings blurred by speed. But hummingbirds have long, needlelike bills; hummingbird moths do not.

 KINGFISHERS (*Alcedinidae*)

Expert divers with big heads, shaggy crests, and long, pointy bills that make up a third of the bird's length. Kingfishers hover over or sit on strategic perches above fish-filled water, then plunge, bill first, often submerging themselves in the process. The pigeon-sized Belted Kingfisher is one of the most widespread birds in North America. The larger (crow-sized) but similar Ringed Kingfisher and

You may mistake it for an insect, but it is unlikely you will mistake a hummingbird for any other North American bird species. Shown here is a female Ruby-throated Hummingbird, the only hummingbird species that breeds in the East.

much smaller (starling-sized) Green Kingfisher are more geographically restricted, residing mostly in South Texas (also southeastern Arizona for Green Kingfisher).

Flamboyant and very vocal. Both Belted and Ringed Kingfishers commonly call as soon as they see you. Green Kingfisher, which often perches very close to banks and the water, makes its presence known with sharp ticking calls.

 ## WOODPECKERS (*Picidae*)

A fairly large, distinctive bird group characterized by chisel-like bills and short, stiff tails that, along with their very specialized feet, serve to anchor the birds against tree trunks and limbs. Woodpeckers range from the sparrow-sized Downy Woodpecker to the crow-sized Pileated Woodpecker, with most falling between the size of a starling and a robin. Most are boldly patterned, black (or brown) and white, and most have eye-catching patches of red on the head and face (the females of some species lack the red, however, and two northern species have yellow, not red, crowns).

Their habit of hitching themselves up the trunks of trees is almost unique. In North America, only the tiny, all-brown Brown Creeper has a similar feeding pattern. The jackhammer action of woodpeckers' bills is unique, too, but it is not the bird's only method of foraging. Some woodpeckers snap insects out of the air. Some root in the ground. Some flake bark off trees. Many pluck and consume berries and acorns.

Usually solitary, but the species that maintain territories all year commonly stay within sight or sound of a mate. Some woodpeckers join winter flocks, moving through woodland with chickadees, titmice, nuthatches, and kinglets. Not all woodpeckers are bound to mature trees. Downy Woodpeckers commonly forage among reeds or tall weeds. Ladder-backed Woodpeckers forage in dry brush lands, on desert cactus, and on the ground.

Nuthatches are sometimes mistaken for woodpeckers, but nuthatches are more frenetic and maneuver on trees by hitching themselves both up and down. Woodpeckers can only climb.

FLYCATCHERS (*Tyrannidae*): Pewees, *Empidonax* Flycatchers, *Myiarchus* Flycatchers, Kingbirds

A large and diverse group united (for the most part) by their ability to fly out from a fixed perch and snap up insect prey. Not all of them take insects out of the air, however (many *Empidonax* flycatchers, or Empids, pluck them from leaves and branches). And not all consume insects year-round. Eastern Kingbird, for example, switches over to a fruit diet in winter (even in migration).

Pewees are dark, somewhat peak-headed forest flycatchers that like open perches in mature trees. Empids are small, generally greenish or gray backed, and generally high-strung, twitchy, and nervous. *Myiarchus* flycatchers are larger, calmer, and more colorful, with brownish upperparts, grayish bibs, and yellowish underparts. Kingbirds are open-country specialists, sitting in a prominent place (often the highest perch around) then zipping out to take insects out of the air or on the ground (or snap a berry off a vine).

Other species also sally out and snap insects out of the air, including gulls, mimids, warblers, even House Sparrow. Flycatchers hunt from perches, however, returning there to wait and watch.

 SHRIKES (*Laniidae*)

They look like mockingbirds, they hunt like raptors. Two species are found in North America, the widespread Loggerhead Shrike and the Northern Shrike. Mostly gray with black masks and short, hooked bills, shrikes sit on high, exposed perches in open country, searching for prey that ranges in size from grasshoppers to small birds.

Smaller birds generally ignore mockingbirds, but they scold shrikes.

VIREOS (*Vireonidae*)

Basically, short-range shrikes. A small, warbler-sized family of mostly forest- and brush-loving birds that hop deliberately through foliage, plucking insects and caterpillars from leaves. Small, fairly large headed, and (mostly) short tailed, vireos appear generally more compact or robust than warblers. Short, thickish bills with a tiny hook at the tip like those of shrikes. Not particularly striking or colorful (Black-capped Vireo excepted), most vireos are dark, somewhat grayish backed and pale, often yellowish or with traces of yellow below. Some species have a "spectacled" face pattern; some are capped. Some have bold wing bars; some do without.

Commonly vocalize as they move about. They also tend to land on sturdier twigs and branches than their lighter and more nimble warbler cousins.

Easily confused with several warbler species, most notably Pine Warbler.

 CROWS AND JAYS (*Corvidae*)

A common, distinctive, animated, vocal, and—because of all this—familiar bird group. Crows and ravens are large, black birds of open and semi-open country. Jays are, for the most part, forest or woodland birds that move like colorful troops through their territories. Exceptions are Clark's Nutcrackers, which often forage above the timber line, and magpies, which favor open country dotted with trees. All have loud, distinctive calls and are, at most times of the year, very vocal.

LARKS (*Alaudidae*)

A group of small, thin-billed birds of open, often sparsely vegetated and unvegetated, habitat (e.g., beaches and plowed fields). In North America, this family is represented by the abundant and wide-spread Horned Lark and the Sky Lark, introduced to Vancouver Island, British Columbia. Seldom landing on trees or bushes, the birds forage by shuffling or running. In winter, they are frequently found in large flocks.

In winter, larks often associate with longspurs and Snow Bunting.

SWALLOWS (*Hirundinidae*)

Small, nimble, petite-billed aerial acrobats that snatch insects out of thin air. Fairly compact bodies are borne aloft by long, pointy, backward-angled wings that give birds the appearance (and maneuverability) of tiny jet fighters. Tails are fairly short and notched (on perched birds, folded wings project well beyond the tails), but Barn Swallows have long, elegantly tined tails. Mostly dark (green, blue, brown) above, white below. Many species have iridescent upperparts; the entire body of male Purple Martins is glossy purple.

Highly social. Commonly forage, nest, and roost in colonies. In migration, and in winter, roosts may number in the tens, even hundreds, of thousands. Often seen perched shoulder to shoulder on utility lines.

CHICKADEES, TITMICE (*Paridae*), AND ALLIES (Verdins, Bushtits)

Tiny, petite-billed acrobats of trees and woodland. Plump-bodied, long-tailed—titmice have crests; chickadees have round, mostly black-capped heads and bibbed throats. Black, white, and gray are tribal colors; some species are washed or enhanced with touches of chestnut. The closely related Verdin has a yellow head and hard-to-see touch of rust on the shoulder. Also closely related, the Bushtit, a slight, long-tailed sprite of a bird, is overall plain and almost always found in flocks.

Very social, foraging in groups (that often include other members of this family as well as other species). Endearingly tame, entertaining, and acrobatic. Commonly dangle upside down and come readily to offerings of sunflower seed and suet.

 ## NUTHATCHES (*Sittidae*)

Small, chunky, neckless, tail-less, avian windup toys that clamber jerkily up, down, and around tree trunks and branches. Blue-gray above with contrasting caps; white (some with touches of rust or a rusty wash) below. All have thin, pointy, nutpicklike bills that they use to pry into crevices.

Movements are jerky and nonstop. In winter, often found among troops of chickadees and kinglets. Sometimes land on the ground, but members of this group are most partial to mature trees, with species occurring in a variety of forests and woodland.

BROWN CREEPER (*Certhiidae*)

A small, brown, wrenlike bird with a thin, down-turned bill and a woodpecker's tail. Hitches itself up tree trunks with jerky movements.

 WRENS (*Troglodytidae*)

Small, brown, furtive, and mostly ground- and vegetation-hugging birds with big voices. Overall plumpish, neckless birds with slender, down-turned bills and tails of varying length that are often up-cocked. Mostly brown and subtly patterned above, paler and sometimes spotted or barred below. Most show a pale or white eyebrow.

Some species are at home in barren, rocky terrain; some are brush or understory skulkers. Rarely do wrens range high in taller trees; never do these birds occur in flocks. Move by hops and short flights. Commonly disappear then reappear on an elevated, open perch (as if to taunt you). Nervous, jerky, animated, and vocal. Songs are often loud and ringing: some elaborate, others comical.

 AMERICAN DIPPER (*Cinclidae*)

A medium-sized, plump, gray, short-tailed bird often seen standing on rocks in fast-rushing streams into which it dives and swims, submerged.

Nimble, acrobatic, often showing an up-cocked tail and a slender, slightly down-turned bill. Lots of wrens, including the Marsh Wren, fit this description. Why not? They're all wrens.

RED-WHISKERED BULBUL (*Pycnonotidae*)

Introduced from Asia and found in the Miami, Florida, area. Resembles a brown-backed, pale-breasted cardinal.

 ### KINGLETS (*Regulidae*)

Tiny, hyperactive birds that maneuver among branches and short-needle confers; frequently hovering and wing-flicking nervously, they look and behave like tiny, short-tailed chickadees. Mostly grayish green—contrasting plumage details are often hard to note. Often join chickadee flocks. Commonly vocalize as they forage: Golden-crowned Kinglets make high-pitched *tsee* notes, and Ruby-crowned Kinglets make a two-part stutter: *j'jiit*.

 ### OLD WORLD WARBLERS (*Sylviidae*)

A group of mostly small, plain, brush-loving birds whose sole breeding representative in North America is the Arctic Warbler of Alaska.

GNATCATCHERS (*Polioptilinae*)

Tiny, pale, slender, long-tailed wisps of a bird that dance among twigs in woodland, chaparral, and desert brush. Resemble miniature mockingbirds with thin bills; long, narrow tails that they swish from side to side; and staring, white-ringed eyes. Overall grayish above, whitish below, with a darker, blackish tail. In some species, males sport a blackish cap.

Flight—on short, rounded wings—is weak. Sometimes hover momentarily and sometimes fly to the ground then quickly back to the surrounding foliage.

 THRUSHES (*Turdidae*): Bluethroats, Northern Wheatears, Bluebirds, Townsend's Solitaires, Robins, Spot-breasted Thrushes, et al.

A diverse group of small- to medium-sized songbirds of forests and open country that commonly sing from high perches but mostly forage for insects and fruit in the understory or, very commonly, on the ground. Compact, sometimes plumpish or portly, with stout, straight bills; an alert, heads-up stance; and tails that often seem just a little short. Commonly move across the ground with springy hops followed by a studied pause. Some species hunt from perches, often close to the ground. Also sally out to pluck fruit or berries from vines and branches. Many in this group, including American Robin, are celebrated for their elegiac whistled or harmonic songs. In winter, some species (bluebirds, robins) gather in flocks.

WRENTIT (*Timaliidae*)

A small, long-tailed chaparral skulker found only along the West Coast.

 ### MIMIDS (*Mimidae*): Catbirds, Mockingbirds, Thrashers

Medium-sized, brush-loving songbirds, recognized by their mostly down-turned bills and long tails. Celebrated for their marathon singing sessions that often incorporate snatches of songs from other bird species. Commonly sing from elevated (often the highest) perches; forage for the most part on or close to the ground and are very adept at staying hidden. Not particularly colorful—some species are gray or grayish; most are brown with plain or streaked or spotted breasts. When singing, mimids are mostly erect. When foraging, they often crouch with their heads lower than their tails.

 ### STARLINGS AND MYNAS (*Sturnidae*)

Old World species introduced to North America. The ubiquitous European Starling is a compact, straight-billed, short-tailed, mostly dark bird found in a variety of open habitats, particularly those altered by our species. Adults in summer shine with rainbow iridescence. In winter, brown above; heavily spotted below. Young are all dull brown.

Starlings thrive in cities and in suburbia. They infest cattle feedlots and open landfills. Commonly seen foraging on lawns and perched on utility lines but also forage on mudflats with shorebirds and sally forth and snap insects out of the air. Roost in large flocks,

Mimids, like this Brown Thrasher, are celebrated and near-tireless singers.

often beneath bridges or in nooks and crannies of buildings. In flight, when hawks are present, starlings often coalesce into tightly packed, wheeling flocks that flash, like puffs of smoke.

Common Myna and Hill Myna are found principally in southern Florida.

WAGTAILS AND PIPITS (*Motacillidae*)

Small, slender, petite, pointy-billed, and long-tailed ground-dwelling birds of open country that nervously jerk their heads or wag their tails as they walk. Wagtails, rarely seen outside Western Alaska, are strikingly patterned. Pipits are cryptically brown, with streaked underparts. They winter in extensive grassland and plowed fields and on beaches. American Pipit, the more common and widespread species, gathers in large flocks that seem to melt into plowed fields without a trace.

 WAXWINGS (*Bombycilidae*)

Medium-sized, elegant, treetop-perching songbirds, shaped somewhat like a starling but adorned with a rakish, swept-back crest. Overall caramel colored with highlighting touches of white, black, yellow, and red; young birds are streaked below. Commonly perch on the highest branches of trees, most commonly in the company of other waxwings. Often betray their presence by emitting a high, trilling sigh.

 PHAINOPEPLA (*Ptilogonatidae*)

Medium-sized, mostly treetop (or brush-top) bird that resembles an elongated, black waxwing with a sparse, disheveled crest. Often sits conspicuously high. Limited to the Southwest, Phainopepla is the sole North American member of this tropical family.

WOOD-WARBLERS (*Parulidae*)

A very large family composed mostly of small, agile, usually arboreal species that hop through foliage, searching for insects. Bills are short and pointy. In many species, males (also some females) are brightly colored. Songs are generally short but rich and engaging. Some species forage on or near the ground, some are mid-story or treetop specialists, some snatch prey out of the air. Most retreat into Central and South America in winter. A few remain in North America, and some augment their diet with berries.

Warblers are a very large family of small, mostly forest birds known for their vocalizations and striking plumage (even, as in the case of this female Black-and-White Warbler, when the palette is somewhat limited).

 TANAGERS (*Thraupidae*)

Colorful, vocal, medium-sized woodland birds that resemble robust, heavy-billed warblers. Males are strikingly colored (all North American species show, at the very least, reddish heads); females are yellowish. Tanagers forage for the most part in the forest canopy, moving about by hopping or making short flights. Some also hover and fly-catch. Whistled songs are rich and somewhat robinlike.

 SPARROWS (*Emberizidae*), including Towhees, Juncos

A very large family of small, conical-billed, mostly ground-foraging species that make a fashion statement with the color brown. Males and females in this group are typically identical or similar. Unless singing from exposed perches, sparrows are commonly hidden, foraging in tall grass, the forest floor, low brush, or scrub. Different species occupy a wide variety of habitat—in fact, almost all terrestrial habitats. While brown is a common color along sparrows, many are richly and distinctly patterned, some touched with color, and a few brightly colored (such as the Spotted Towhee). Some species hop, others walk or run.

CARDINALS (*Cardinalidae*), including Grosbeaks, Buntings

A diverse group of small- to medium-sized, heavy, conical-billed birds. Males and females/juveniles in this group have very different plumages, with males being very colorful and or strikingly patterned. Larger grosbeaks are mostly forest and canopy birds. Sparrow-sized buntings prefer edges and open areas with varying amounts of vegetation and commonly feed on or near the ground. The crested Northern Cardinal and Pyrrhuloxia are distinctive. Males in this group are very vocal. Whistled songs are mostly rich and cheery. Call notes are refreshingly distinctive.

 ## BLACKBIRDS, OR ICTERIDS (*Icteridae*), including Bobolinks, Meadowlarks, Blackbirds, Grackles, Cowbirds, Orioles

A fairly large and distinctly two-sided family: colorful and not. Bills are pointy and fairly short but vary in length from species to species. Bobolink, meadowlarks, and orioles are on the colorful side; blackbirds, grackles, and cowbirds are mostly black (or brown), but their plumages often show iridescence, and some male blackbirds have distinct and colorful adornments (the red epaulets on Red-winged Blackbird, for example).

Bobolink, meadowlarks, and most blackbirds are grassland or marsh specialists. Orioles are arboreal. Many in this group are gifted vocalists (the blackbirds, for the most part, excepted). In migration, winter, and (with some species) the breeding season, highly gregarious; many species form flocks, some large.

Icterids include blackbirds and orioles, and while many are gifted singers, the vocalizations of the male Boat-tailed Grackle tend to be comical and histrionic.

FINCHES (*Fringillidae*), including Rosy-Finches, Crossbills, Siskins, Goldfinches, Pine and Evening Grosbeaks

A group of mostly tree-loving birds of northern forests. Most have short, conical bills (crossbills excepted). Most are agile seedeaters, able to move nimbly about the outer branches of seed-bearing trees (including birches and conifers). Goldfinches and redpolls also forage on weed seeds close to the ground). The birds are easily attracted to bird-feeding stations. Outside the breeding season, they commonly occur in large, vocal flocks. Often seen picking grit from roadsides. In flight, birds undulate. Flocks are globular and shifting.

 OLD WORLD SPARROWS (*Passeridae*)

The introduced but widespread House Sparrow and very restricted (to the St. Louis, Missouri, area) Eurasian Tree Sparrow are the sole representatives of this family in North America.

4 Getting Real, Getting Focused, Getting to the Right Seat

By the time I was ten, I'd outgrown that early pocket field guide that left me so habitat challenged. What replaced it was not a field guide at all but a two-volume set published by the National Geographic Society that was information rich but illustration impoverished. The photos and illustrations (and supporting text) were never intended to be like those in an identification guide. Nevertheless, it's what I had so it's what I used.

Indoors, of course. The large hardcover books were never intended to be taken into the field. So what I would do is wander around in the woodland behind my parents' house. Find and then study birds with my binoculars. And when I saw a bird I didn't know (which was pretty often), study it until I had its image emblazoned in my mind then run home before the memory faded.

I was actually pretty good at it. First, because as a member of the hominid family, I have a brain that is hot-wired for study and recognition. The other reason I was pretty good at noting detail was because, like many of the members of my generation, I received special training. I was an avid fan of a children's television show called *Romper Room* (sort of the precursor to *Sesame Street*).

One of the show's teaching exercises was "One, Two, Three— Look and See." It worked like this: The show's host would display a board upon which she'd placed a half dozen or so stick-on images: cow, pig, farmer, watering can, chicken, straw hat.

After a brief period of study, she'd close a curtain over the array, slyly reach her hand behind the curtain, remove an element or two, then draw back the curtain with the challenge, "One, two, three—look and see."

You had to look at the board and try to determine which element (or elements) she'd removed. If you beat the gaggle of kids sitting in the studio, you won.

I really liked "One, Two, Three—Look and See." By the time I got around to looking at birds and noting details, I was already in the upper decile of my class when it came to seeing and remembering stuff.

Where am I going with this? Two places. First, I didn't fall into the easy trap set for most beginning birders. I didn't have a field guide with me, so I was never tempted to use valuable field time flipping through pages trying to identify a bird sitting in front of me. I spent my field time studying and trying to memorize the bird.

Common Yellowthroat was one of the very first birds I ever identified. The adult male's black bandit's mask, the classic field mark touted in many field guides, was a dead giveaway.

Second, I never looked at birds from the standpoint of noting individual parts—i.e., I never lost track of the *whole* bird. Sure, I learned the importance of, and learned to note, key and distinguishing characteristics, the "field marks." But the lesson of "One, Two, Three—Look and See" was to recognize and remember whole animals. Only classic field guides tell you to remember parts.

The size and shape of the bill, shape and pattern of the face and head, presence or absence of wing bars or spots or steaks on the underparts, length of the legs and shape of the feet, shape and length of the tail—these were the characteristics that birders used to distinguish one species from the next. They were touted in field guides as *the* way to identify a bird (first note details!).

But by focusing on the bird and not the parts, I was able to see and appreciate the bird in its entirety. Size, shape, posture, manner of locomotion . . . all the things, we have come to learn, that can be as important in distinguishing one species from the next as are details relating to plumage.

Some field guides will tell you to study birds systematically. Start at the beak, then the head, then the back and wings, then the underparts and legs and feet, then the tail. Some authors will encourage birders to draw new and unfamiliar species—both as an exercise for noting details and as a record, for later, in case memory fails. Some will enjoin you to simply look at the whole bird.

What all these methods—systematic, field sketch, and holistic—have in common is the encouragement to use field time for study.

Look at the bird. Note everything about it. Train yourself to perceive, automatically, distinguishing characteristics—those tent-pole traits that are the primary focus of most field guides. But don't lose track of the big picture. Note behavioral characteristics, too. Does the bird walk or hop? Does it move slowly and methodically or quickly and furtively? Does it wag its tail or bob its head or flick its wings or perch upright or slouch? You never know what traits are going to be useful, even determining, so note everything.

Most of all, use field time for study. Keep the guide closed, the app off. There will be plenty of time later for matching what you saw with the image in your guide.

When to Say Wren

So you've taken me up on my challenge and are in your backyard, hunting up birds so you can learn more about them and develop a more family-focused search image.

And sure enough, you run into a bird you're unfamiliar with and can't identify.

Happens all the time. Welcome to birding.

You have already started the identification process. You've noted the habitat. Suburban yard. Corner section. Near the fence and the neighbor's old wooden shed. Dominant vegetation: grass, rosebushes, ivy, rank weeds along the fence (note to self—got to clean this corner up), overhanging shade trees. You are aware of the season, if not the date. Let's say it's summer.

And while you may not recognize the tiny, brown, furtive bird in front of you, you have already pared away a lot of possibilities, birds you know it is not. Albatross, duck, crow, hawk, flicker . . .

If not yet, then pretty soon, it is going to be evident that this tiny, brown mote of feathered energy falls into that large group of birds that includes a number of families (and takes up almost half of your field guide). This large scientific order is called the "perching birds." It incorporates a number of families: flycatchers, swallows, thrushes, warblers, sparrows . . .

"Sparrow," you think. "It's small and brown like most sparrows, but . . ."

Small and Brown, But . . .

Let's review. Your experience with birds (i.e., your familiarization with sparrows) and your powers of perception have brought you this far and no farther.

You are looking at a small, brown bird. From among the birds you are most familiar with, it's most like a sparrow. Good jumping-off point. But don't reach for your field guide and start flipping through the sparrow section. Remember: Use field time for study. It's time to bring binoculars and your focus to bear and start assimilating clues. Be observant—note everything. Be creative—relate what you see to things you are familiar with.

Things to note:

Size? Small. Really small. In fact, tiny—somewhere between a hummingbird and a chickadee.

Shape? Funny looking. Pickle shaped. Somewhat neckless.

Bill? Fairly short, slightly down-turned, and thin. Looks a bit like a nutpick.

Face pattern? Kind of blah, nothing. Maybe a pale line over the eye. Otherwise, pretty plain.

Tail? Fairly long, but shorter than the body is long and straight and narrow. Popsicle-stick wide with a rounded tip. Sometimes tail is slightly up-cocked, sometimes lowered, making the bird look tired or dejected.

Legs? Short. Hard to see. Pinkish gray.

Color? Overall brown above. No distinctive field marks (no bold plumage patterns). Dirty white throat going to pale brown below. Wings and tail show narrow, indistinct, dark bands. Some faint banding on the sides, too.

Movements? Quick, nervous, jerky. Rarely still for long. Doesn't seem to like landing on the ground. Moves through vegetation by making short hops or flies short distances. When searching for food, seems to travel up and down as much or more than side to side. Very tame.

Flight? Fast and direct with rapid, constant wing beats that are too fast to count. Flight recalls a bumblebee.

Yes, it's a lot to note. But since you are dealing with an unfamiliar bird, you never know what hints or clues are going to be important, even determining. And even though you may still not know what this bird is, you now know a great deal about it. More than enough to identify it correctly. In fact, and I hate to say this, more than many very experienced birders—birders who focus exclusively on field marks—know.

And, if you really are somewhat familiar with sparrows, somewhere in the study of the bird in front of you, you began to realize that it is *not* a sparrow.

Size: Many sparrows are small and brown, but most species are not tiny like this bird.

Shape: Most sparrows have plumpish bodies with heads that are distinct from the body and proportionally long tails. This bird's head and body seem fused and wedge shaped, not like a sparrow's.

Small and brown. It could be a sparrow. But while Song Sparrow is one of the most common and widespread species in North America, it is not the only small, brown bird in town. Look again.

Bill/face pattern: Most sparrows have a fairy discernible face pattern, and, most of all, sparrows have bills that are short and conical—like a capital V fixed to the bird's face. Nutpick shaped hardly describes a sparrow's bill.

Behavior: Most sparrows spend a lot of time foraging on or near the ground. This bird seems reluctant to let its feet touch the earth.

So what you are left with is a small, nimble, furtive, pickle-shaped, brown, largely patternless bird with a nutpick bill that spends most of its time creeping through vegetation. And when you go through the field guide, you'll find a family of birds that fits this description perfectly: the wrens.

Finding the Right Seat

Wrens. "Small, brown and active but secretive; they creep through vegetation" is the description given by David Sibley at the beginning of the wrens section of his field guide.

OK. You are in the right section, even row (wrens are a family)—or at least you think you are. The bird, you suspect, is a wren. Now comes the final step—determining what species of wren. And what you are going to learn about wrens is something that is pretty typical of bird identification. It is easy to narrow down the search to two or three species but hard to pick a champion.

From Broad Brush to Fine Details

There are ten species of wrens in North America, all fundamentally alike. (Why not? They're all wrens.) And while most are brownish and fairly cryptically colored, there are, when you study the plates, only three that are patently, in fact, distinctly, plain—mostly devoid of eye-catching field marks.

House Wren, Winter Wren, and Pacific Wren. (If your guide doesn't show Pacific Wren, don't panic. Until recently, the bird was considered a type of Winter Wren, a subspecies, which are in essence regional forms of a species. Differences are slight—so slight that the biggest difference is usually geographic. One subspecies is found here, another there.)

Plumage-wise, House, Winter, and Pacific Wrens are pretty similar: plain and brown, with House Wren the plainest of the lot. But look at their shapes. The bird you saw had a pickle-shaped body with a fairly long tail—like a House Wren. Winter and Pacific Wrens are tiny, plump-bodied birds with very short, vertically cocked tails, abbreviated nubs of tails. They look like feathered ping-pong balls with a pencil stub for a tail.

So probably not a Winter or Pacific Wren.

You now have a champion. A candidate. A theory. But not a winner. Not yet. You think the bird might be a House Wren. Now test the theory.

Look at the range map in your field guide. You'll discover that House Wren is very widespread across North America (Central and South America, too), breeding as far north as southern Canada and much of the United States. And because range maps are usually color coded, they show not only the range of a species but its seasonal distribution. While some species are permanent residents, many others are not. House Wren, for instance, vacates its northern breeding ranges in winter. Between November and March, a House

Wren in Ohio would be temporally out of bounds, disqualified by the season. So a small, brown, plain wren seen in winter in Ohio should prompt you to reevaluate your initial assessment. Winter Wren (as the name implies) is a much more likely candidate than House Wren.

If range and seasonality check out, confirm that the habitat in which you found the bird conforms with the description in the book. "Shrubs, farms, gardens, parks." Sounds promising.

Finally, many field guides will also tell you whether a bird is common or uncommon, or scarce or rare. While a bird's abundance is not determining, it is, from the perspective of a beginning birder trying to pin names to unfamiliar birds, very reassuring. Most of the birds you will encounter in the early stages of birding (and the advanced stages, too) are going to be common.

Winter Wren and Pacific Wren? You'll want to check the distribution for them as well, and what you'll discover is that these two species have more restricted ranges and that both birds are, over

It might not be sitting on a birdhouse, but the bird pictured here is no less a House Wren. Commit the bird's size, shape, and mannerisms to memory and you learn to spell W-R-E-N.

most of those ranges, woodland birds, with a particular fondness for mature trees.

Everything about this bird agrees with the identification of House Wren, one of the most common and widespread species in North America.

Congratulations. Not only have you found a new species but you just became familiar with another bird family. Knowing House Wren has brought you to a familiarity with wrens in general. When you see a Winter Wren, or Carolina Wren, or Bewick's Wren, or Rock Wren, your powers of recognition will jump-start your identification. The next time you see a wren, you'll start the identification process by going right to the wren section of your mind and searching for the right seat.

Finally In the Right Seat and Settling In

Now you've got your field guide out. You've studied the plate, read the description, and are satisfied with the identification.

If you are really serious about learning how to identify birds, and if the bird is still in view, continue watching it. It's a Life Bird. A new bird for you. Pinning a name to it is just the first step, the ante that gets you into the game. Now it's time to increase your familiarity.

In a sense, all you've really done so far is learn to spell House Wren. Learned that small size; small, nutpick-shaped bill; neckless, pickle-shaped body; shortish, straight tail; and quick, furtive movements are the letters in the bird alphabet that spell H-O-U-S-E W-R-E-N.

In many ways, learning to identify birds is analogous to learning to spell, or, more accurately, to read. The various traits or field marks—body shape, leg length, bill shape and length, tail shape and length, color, pattern—are like the letters of an alphabet. You put them together, and they spell an identification.

H-O-U-S-E W-R-E-N.

What I suggest you do now is summarize all the elements of the encounter. Put your wren in a sentence, a sentence that summarizes all the elements of your encounter with the bird.

"In late June, in _____, I saw a House Wren foraging with quick, jerky movements in the low bushes and ivy for insects using a combination of short hops and short flights, often disappearing into the vegetation and flying finally in a direct line, on rapid wing beats, less than five feet above the ground."

Yes, it's a lousy, run-on sentence, but it puts your bird in context. A bird in a plate in a field guide is a disembodied thing. Static. Lifeless. A bird in the field is an element in a tapestry—a tapestry that not only supports its being there but even determines it!

Why is this holistic approach important? Because not only have you moved from identifying a bird to recognizing it, you have just established a search image for this species, a context.

You don't just know what House Wren looks like. You know how it behaves, how it moves, what habitat it favors, what flavor of ice cream it likes.

OK, I'm kidding about the ice cream. Just testing to see if you are really reading this.

Luckily, your first contact with this species was protracted. You had all the time you needed to make a correct identification. But what if next time all you get is a glimpse of a small, furtive, brown bird that disappears and doesn't reappear? No bland facial pattern discerned. No telltale nutpick-shaped bill to support your identification.

Well, if you have all the other elements in place—the matrix that supports the identification "House Wren"—you have the rest of the sentence. All you need to do is fill in the blank.

Hmmm, I just saw a [small, furtive, brown bird] foraging with quick, jerky movements in low bushes and ivy and, after a couple of short hops and a short flight, it disappeared into the vegetation.

Actually, there is no *hmmm* about it. Because of your acquired familiarity with House Wren, taken in the context of the particulars relating to your newest encounter, your mind will automatically call up "House Wren," filling in the blank with the name.

This, by the way, is how experienced birders do it—relying as much on memory and context as visual content. The more you know, the quicker and surer your identification will be. And yes, you are a long way from being an experienced birder. But the way to become experienced is by gathering experience. And now that you've added House Wren to your index of familiar species, you are one bird and one family group closer to being the experienced birder you want to be.

Oh, one other thing, you have also just sown the seeds for one of the greatest pitfalls in birding. More on that later.

So, time to close the book on House Wren and move on to something else? Not yet.

Build On It

The problem with a field guide is the name. It implies that a field guide is intended to be used in the field, which in fact most are. But field guides don't just come into play when you have engaged a bird in the field. Studying them *before* you go into the field helps prepare you to know what field marks are important to note when glimpses are brief. They are also extremely useful *after* you have seen a bird. They serve to review and recap what you noted in the field, making it easier to bring this knowledge to bear again, later.

When I was just learning my birds, I used to sit in bed and read through the species accounts. Look at the illustration, read the text. Look at the next illustration, read the text.

It helped.

But one of the things I discovered about trying to learn field marks on birds I'd yet to see was how hard it was to retain the information. I'd read an account, and forget almost everything I'd just read before I was halfway through the next one. So in time I developed the habit of reading everything I could about a bird *after* my first encounter with it.

Before a first encounter with a species, it's an abstraction, no different from any other unfamiliar bird in the guide's plates. I could appreciate it—I just couldn't bond to it. After I'd seen the bird, however, it became real. I could relate. And I wanted—really wanted—to know everything about it.

So the evening after a first encounter with a new species, I'd read everything I could find about the bird. Every account in every field guide. Every natural history description. Using this technique, I found I could assimilate information in a fraction of the time (and get to savor my encounter anew).

Just think! If you discovered, studied, and assimilated all there is to know about just one bird a day, in less than two years, you would be familiar with every breeding bird in North America north of the Rio Grande.

A SELECTION OF BIRDING RESOURCES

Bird Identification's Triple Crown

These three guides (two illustrated, one photo driven) complement each other and deserve to be in every birder's library (and you'll probably want a second set for the car).

Kaufman Field Guide to Birds of North America. Kenn Kaufman. Houghton Mifflin Harcourt, 2005.

Arguably the best introductory, photo-driven field guide to North American birds available.

The Sibley Guide to Birds. David Allen Sibley. Knopf, 2000.

A brilliantly conceived, thoughtfully organized, illustration-driven guide.

National Geographic Field Guide to the Birds of North America, Sixth Edition. Jon L. Dunn and Jonathan Alderfer. National Geographic, 2011.

The "Geo Guide" is a comprehensive, all-inclusive, illustrated field guide that gives full coverage to all regional forms.

Other Recommended General Field Guides (in Random Order)

While one field guide is destined to serve as your primary guide, additional resources offer unique information and are invaluable when the identification process comes down to a choice between two closely related candidates. Birds of Europe is a superb guide, and remember: Many species of birds found in Europe also occur in North America.

Birds of Eastern North America. Paul Sterry and Brian E. Small. Princeton University Press, 2009.

Smithsonian Field Guide to the Birds of North America. Ted Floyd. Harper Collins, 2008.

Stokes Field Guide to the Birds of North America. Donald and Lillian Stokes. Little, Brown and Company, 2010.

National Wildlife Federation Field Guide to Birds of North America. Edward S. Brinkley. Sterling, 2007.

American Museum of Natural History Birds of North America Eastern Region [and *Western Region*]. Francois Vuilleumier, editor. DK Publishing, 2011.

Birds of Europe, Second Edition. Lars Svensson, Dan Zetterstrom, and Killian Mullarney. Princeton University Press, 2010.

Specialty Guides That Support and Advance Your Skills

Basic field guides are squeezed for space. These guides offer additional identification hints and clues that are most helpful with challenging bird groups such as shorebirds and birds of prey.

Pete Dunne's Essential Field Guide Companion. Pete Dunne. Houghton Mifflin Harcourt, 2006.

The Shorebird Guide. Michael O'Brien, Richard Crossley, and Kevin Karlson. Houghton Mifflin Harcourt, 2006.

Hawks at a Distance. Jerry Liguori. Princeton University Press, 2011.

Kaufman Field Guide to Advanced Birding. Kenn Kaufman. Houghton Mifflin Harcourt, 2011.

Hawks in Flight, Second Edition. Pete Dunne, David Sibley, and Clay Sutton. Houghton Mifflin Harcourt, 2012.

Books That Go Beyond Field Identification

A field guide description is a sketch, the skeleton of a bird. These books put flesh and feathers on the bones, offering insights into the birds themselves.

Lives of North American Birds. Kenn Kaufman. Houghton Mifflin Harcourt, 1996.

Ornithology, Third Edition. Frank B. Gill. W.H. Freeman, 2006.

The Birder's Handbook. Paul R. Ehrlich, David S. Dobkin, and Darryl Wheye. Simon & Schuster, 1988.

The Birdwatcher's Companion to North American Birdlife. Christopher W. Leahy. Princeton University Press, 2004.

The Sibley Guide to Bird Life and Behavior. David Allen Sibley. Knopf, 2009.

The Birds of North America (online series).

A thorough biological treatment of every breeding bird in North America; an invaluable resource for birders available by annual subscription (BNAorders@ebsco.com or 1-877-873-2626).

5 | Picking On Birds Your Own Size

Huse Wren! Pretty tough identification, but there are others just as challenging. Birds such as warblers that are, like wrens, mostly arboreal but spend a great deal of time way up in the tops of trees. Birds such as *Empidonax* flycatchers, which look maddeningly alike, or hawks, which rarely let observers get close enough to see distinguishing characteristics and are often viewed heading dead away in flight.

Which offer birders a whole 'nother set of identification challenges.

And opportunities.

One of the proven ways to get your basic identification skill set down is to practice on birds that play fair. Birds that are large, sedentary, and not particularly skittish. Birds that spend a great deal of time in the open and whose distinguishing characteristics are bold and easily noted.

There are a couple of groups of birds that meet this standard: the herons (and heronlike birds) and waterfowl—ducks and geese.

Both groups are, for the most part, birds associated with water and in the proper habitat can be common, even abundant. Herons and egrets, as wading birds, tend to be in shallow water or along the shorelines of larger lakes, ponds, and impoundments. Ducks forage in shallow and deeper water (in fact, are divided into two groups, dabblers and divers, exploiting different water depths).

The point is that both these groups are widespread and easy to find and study. They are also often found in places that attract lots

Of course bird identification is challenging. That's why it's so much fun. This fairly typical view of an Orange-crowned Warbler offers a challenge to many an experienced birder.

of birders (such as parks and refuges) so the birds are habituated to people. In addition, in places where herons and waterfowl concentrate, there are commonly multiple species, offering both challenge and gratification and . . .

Here's the best part. Many waterfowl are easy to identify (and, owing to their plumage, gratifying to look at). Among ducks, males tend to be brightly plumaged and show an abundance of classic field marks. It's hard to tear your eyes away from the feast of colors found on a drake Northern Shoveler or Green-winged Teal or Red-breasted Merganser in order to focus on differences relating to size and structure—but you should and you must if you are going to learn how to distinguish female and juvenile ducks, which are more cryptically plumaged.

But make no mistake, ducks can be challenging, too. Among the diving ducks there are two that are notoriously difficult to distinguish: Greater and Lesser Scaup. Once in the World Series of Birding, the three top teams all studied the same drake scaup. One team said Lesser. The other two said Greater. All were confident.

That's right. Even the experts disagreed.

Leave scaup for later. There's challenge enough on the water. Pitfalls, too.

If It Looks Like a Duck . . . It May Not Be a Duck

So you are studying ducks in a freshwater impoundment. Identifying them, too. Northern Pintail, with the rakish tail. American Wigeon, with the rusty sides and buffy, white crown. Male Blue-winged Teal, with the white crescent moon on its face. And, of course, Mallard. Everybody knows the bird with the Day-Glo green head.

But . . . there is this one duck that's giving you trouble. A small one that is all charcoal-gray with a white bill and just a touch of white on the sides of the tail. There's lots of them among the other ducks. You've gone through the waterfowl plates in your field guide several times, and the closest thing you can find is an all-black duck called Black Scoter, which is, happily, "common."

But on the water, you can't find any female Black Scoters, which are browner—only male birds. That's troubling. And, according to the guide, away from their tundra breeding areas, Black Scoters are supposed to be mostly coastal. That's troubling, too.

And, if the truth be known, the bird that's puzzling you really doesn't look like the picture of a Black Scoter. It's just that Black Scoter is the closest likeness you can find among the waterfowl.

Your problem is fundamental (and, I might add, common), and you've even made this mistake before. The problem is you got off on the wrong foot right at the onset of the identification process, just like you did with the flicker. A webbed foot this time.

You deduced, incorrectly, that the all-dark bird with the white bill was a duck. So you ducked into the waterfowl section and started searching.

Maybe duck? Maybe not. Look at the bill. Seems more chickenlike than ducklike. Or, more accurately, American Coot-like.

The bird isn't a duck. It's an American Coot. A bird more closely related to rails, a group of mostly secretive marsh birds. Not all birds that swim (or, for that matter, quack) are ducks. If you could look at the coot's feet, you'd see that they are not fully webbed like the feet of waterfowl but lobed.

"But you can't see the feet!" you are thinking. "They are underwater."

True. But you can see the bill. It's chickenlike (more accurately, rail-like), not at all ducklike. You started down the wrong path right at the beginning of the identification process. Not surprisingly, your identification went nowhere.

Here's the lesson in this. When you run into a jam and can't identify a bird in the family you presume it is in, go back and start over. Study the bird that is giving you trouble. Pay attention to basic structural characteristics. Pick a family group that is more structurally allied with what you are seeing—in the shape of the bill or body or legs or feet or tail.

In the case of the coot, a bird with a chickenlike bill.

Incidently, there are other birds, members of other families, that are commonly found in the same habitat as ducks. These include loons, grebes, and cormorants. They all swim. They all dive (as do many ducks). But they are not ducks, and bill shape is probably the easiest way to tell that they do not fall into the ranks of waterfowl.

This problem of getting off on the wrong foot, of misjudging a bird's family and going down the wrong identification path, applies equally to land birds.

Ovenbird, a bird of the forest floor, is olive-brown above and spotted below—just like several thrushes. The problem is: Ovenbird is a warbler. You won't find it among the thrushes in your guide.

White-throated Swift is a boldly marked, black-and-white aerialist that sweeps across western skies on narrow, swept-back, pointy wings. Among the swifts, this western species is very easily identified. Unless, of course, you make the mistake of placing it, and looking for its likeness, among the swallows, which are also pointy-winged aerialists that snap up insects on the fly.

Swifts have smooth, curving, sickle-shaped wings. Swallows have wings that are angled back.

Then there are blackbirds and crows! Two bird families differing in a number of anatomical respects but usually, and most obviously, by size. Crows—American, Northwestern, Fish, Tamaulipas—are larger than most of the blackbird species (whose large family group also includes the orioles). Even experienced birders tend to initially separate crows and blackbirds largely, and somewhat cavalierly, by size.

But then a birder runs into Boat-tailed or Great-tailed Grackle, magnum-sized blackbirds whose overall length may exceed that of the American Crow.

I say again: Familiarize yourself with bird families. Recognize the traits that place birds in family groups. Be especially careful when you make your initial broad-brush identification. And when you get in a jam, just can't find the bird you are looking at in the expected family, reboot the process. Look and think again.

6 Taking It All In: Integrate, Integrate, Integrate

When I first learned my birds, field identification was much more basic than it is today. Take egrets—large, white herons that forage, for the most part, in shallow, standing water. The way I learned it, Great Egret was the taller one with the yellow bill; Snowy Egret was the small one with a black bill and yellow feet, or "slippers."

It worked! In no time I could tell these two common, all-white herons apart. But the challenge only begins with Great and Snowy Egrets. They may be the most common and widespread of the white herons but they are not by any means the *only* large, white herons in North America.

In coastal Florida, and along the Gulf of Mexico, you'll find Reddish Egret—which comes in an all-white morph and is intermediate in size between Snowy and Great Egrets. Then there is Little Blue Heron, which is similar in size and shape to Snowy Egret.

"Except it's blue!" you're thinking. Yes, uniformly dark blue, as an adult. The challenge is: Juvenile birds are all white, and they retain this plumage for almost a year.

Finally, there is Cattle Egret, which is slightly smaller than Snowy Egret (but shows a yellow bill like Great Egret), and the white morph of the Great Blue Heron. While limited to South Florida, the "Great White Heron" also has a yellowish bill and so might be mistaken for a Great Egret.

All of these white herons are separable in the field using classic field marks (with a primary focus on bill color and pattern). But

Great Egret and Snowy Egret. One has a black bill; one has a yellow bill. But when it comes to separating the white-plumaged herons, the identification process doesn't end there. In fact, it just begins.

size, structure, and field marks are not the only clues available. It turns out that the different herons and egrets behave differently, too—which makes perfect sense. If birds all exploited the same resources the same way, why bother to have different species?

Great Egrets are stately stalkers. They commonly stand in one place for long periods, waiting for fish to approach them, and move with a slow, stalking stride.

Snowy Egrets are more active, nervous. They move more quickly, more often, striding with quick steps and sometimes darting and turning nimbly.

Little Blue Heron is like Great Egret, a slow stalker and stander. It tends to stand for long periods with neck elevated and thrust slightly forward, head turned slightly askew, with one eye trained on the water.

By comparison, Reddish Egret is a very active, even aggressive, feeder, racing across tidal flats with long strides, often with wings open. Turning quickly, leaping, darting, stabbing the water.

Cattle Egret? A landlubber. This bird is almost never seen standing in the water. It slinks through grass (often behind grazing animals), its head weaving like a snake's.

So despite their similar plumages, all of these white herons/egrets can be distinguished by their feeding behaviors. Behavior is a very useful tool in the bird ID field kit. It vaults distances. It is often easier to note than classic field marks. And it is certainly not limited to herons and egrets. Many bird species have idiosyncratic mannerisms that suggest, even confirm, their identity: a flick of a wing, bob of the head, or wag of the tail.

Great White Heron? OK, you got me. They feed a great deal like Great Egrets—slow and stately. That's the bad news. The good news is that they often feed *with* Great Egrets.

Why is this good news? Because in birding . . .

Size Matters

Many field guides suggest that the first step in the identification process should be an assessment of size, followed by structure (or shape). Nobody would argue that these two qualities are not important—in fact, they are commonly the core traits experienced birders use to quickly place birds in the proper family group before whittling their identification down to species.

But where structural characteristics are more or less constant, a person's perception of size is subject to all kinds of variables: distance, light conditions, backdrop. What this means is that size is often difficult to assess correctly. And a faulty perception of size very commonly leads to a misidentification.

A number of years ago, I was participating in a Christmas Bird Count, an annual survey of birds within a prescribed area conducted around the holiday season. It sounds like work but is actually just a great excuse for birding friends to go out in a "party" and bird all day.

Late in the day, on a stretch of coastal marsh, one of my companions picked up a distant anomaly, trained a spotting scope on it, and proudly announced, "I've got a Great Egret." Common in coastal New Jersey in summer, the bird is very uncommon in winter.

Framed as it was against a stand of Phragmites grass, the very distant white bird did indeed stand egret tall. That didn't make it an egret, however. The bird proved to be an adult Herring Gull standing atop a post concealed by reeds.

Both David Sibley in his *Sibley Guide to Birds* and Kenn Kaufman in his *Field Guide to Advanced Birding* underscore the difficulty inherent in judging size in the field. But their caution applies, for the most part, to individual birds, seen at a distance, without some point of reference. Often, this is not the case. In fact, for some groups of birds, isolation is the exception.

Static ID vs. Dynamic

A few pages back, we discussed the identification of birds using study skins. The identification process applied to such specimens was structure and plumage based. It was also isolated and static, prompting students of birds to regard the identification challenge as a laboratory exercise:

You looked solely at the individual specimen, eliminating variables.

You noted its distinguishing characteristics.

Stop.

But the truth is, in the field, birds are never isolated—never divorced from their surrounding environments. They are also, in many cases, not even alone. Many species are social, found with other birds, other species. This association provides an array of comparative hints and clues that become part of the identification matrix.

Back to the Great White Heron and Great Egret. Yes, both herons are large, stand tall, feed similarly, and usually forage across tidal flats. But a Great White Heron is distinctly larger than a Great Egret. This difference may not leap out at observers when birds are alone, but it is very apparent when the birds are in the same field of view (which they commonly are).

At least it's apparent if you are disciplined to look for such differences—if your identification technique is predicated on integrating all the hints and clues available to you, including direct comparison with nearby species.

Back to the Beginning

When we started this discussion of identification, we established that the first step in the identification process was assessing the habitat around you (and the bird). I'm going to suggest to you that you now broaden the scope of "environment" to include all the birds (and other animals) that are also occupying the same habitat. Proximity to other species not only offers a comparative reference for things like size, shape, plumage, and behavior, it also demonstrates similarities and differences in habitat selection that are useful aids to identification.

Take Least and Semipalmated Sandpipers, for instance. Two very similar species among a group of birds—the small sandpipers—that most beginning birders happily ignore until they gain experience. Semipalmated is very slightly larger, slightly grayer above and whiter below, with a straighter, blunter bill, and (as field guides have pointed out for years) black legs. Least Sandpipers are slightly smaller, browner above, dingier white below (with generally more streaking on the breast), pointier faced (with a pointy, slightly more down-turned bill), and have dingy, yellow legs.

But when the birds are found foraging together, these subtle differences commonly become subordinate and supportive. Among a

Least Sandpiper, the smallest member of the small sandpipers (or peeps) tends to stay out of the water, favoring higher, muddier, even drier habitat than do Semipalmated or Western Sandpipers.

group of Least Sandpipers, the more extensive, whiter underparts of Semipalmated Sandpipers leap out and grab an observer's eye. Amid Semipalmated Sandpipers, Least Sandpiper is the small, drab, brownish thing foraging at the edge of the group, most commonly on mud or dry ground.

Note: The two sandpipers tend to sort themselves according to habitat. Semipalmated Sandpipers commonly keep their feet wet (i.e., they stand in the water or on the wetter portion of a mudflat, closest to the water). Least Sandpipers tend to stay in the higher, drier areas, often away from the water's edge.

It makes sense, really. Being larger, Semipalmateds marginalize their smaller cousin into drier and to what is to them less productive habitat (unless you happen to be a Least Sandpiper, specialized to forage in marginal habitat). Being grayer, Semipalmated is better camouflaged against water; being browner, Least Sandpiper blends in with mud.

In bird identification, as in life, the trick is knowing the tricks.

Probability—the Period at the End of the Sentence. Or the Question Mark.

It was late September when I encountered the pair. They had all the affectations of newly converted birders. Khaki pants, khaki shirts, birder vests, floppy hats, field guide pouch at his side . . . a husband-and-wife team, identically, iconically dressed.

"We just had a hundred fifty Wilson's Phalaropes at Stone Harbor," they announced.

Nothing in their smiles suggested they appreciated the improbable nature of their disclosure. And while there was a part of me that wanted to just say "congratulations" and let it go at that, there was another part, the educator-in-me part, that believes that honesty and accuracy trump being polite.

"Were they, by any chance, in the tidal pond just east of the Wetlands Institute?"

"Yes," they confirmed, delighted that I knew the spot.

"Did you happen to find any Lesser Yellowlegs in the pond with them?"

"No," they assured me, "only Wilson's Phalarope."

Wilson's Phalarope and Lesser Yellowlegs do share basic structural similarities and when not in breeding plumage constitute a challenge for birders with limited shorebird experience—particularly when the birds are sitting out the tide, bunched in a flock, as the shorebirds at the pond mentioned commonly do.

But the mistake the couple made was one of the most basic and, among beginning birders, also the most common. They had failed, after making their initial identification, to give their sighting the litmus test—to take probability into account. Given geographic distribution and time of year, Wilson's Phalarope was a highly unlikely prospect.

An unlikely identification does not mean it is wrong. But it does mean that it would be prudent to give serious regard to alternative possibilities.

"What if I were to tell you that Wilson's Phalarope is a very uncommon migrant in New Jersey, and that by late September, the species is extremely rare? Also that the state maximum for Wilson's Phalarope is less than a dozen birds in one place at one time—and that the day before yesterday, in the pond you mentioned, I had a hundred fifty Lesser Yellowlegs, a species that is common here, now?"

The gentleman didn't hesitate more than a second.

"No," he assured me, "these were Wilson's Phalarope."

"Congratulations," I said. "That is a fantastic sighting."

Testing, Testing

It might be said that I did the couple a disservice by not making a more forceful or persuasive argument, convincing them that, while their misidentification was understandable, it was still wrong. I'll make amends by convincing you.

The likelihood that a bird of a certain species should or should not be someplace is contingent on a number of factors: range (or distribution), time of year, population size, habitat, the species' propensity to wander outside its range, and recent weather patterns or systems. Most of these qualifying considerations are normally referenced in the species accounts in your field guide. If the range map for the species you are advancing as a likely candidate shows that species not to be where you (and the bird) are located; if the map shows the bird's range extends into your region in winter but the date is June 15; if the bird is classified as "rare" or, going back to that most basic of considerations, not found in the habitat where your specimen is located—then little red warning flags should be going up in your mind.

Probability is, of course, not determining. Birds *do* wander and turn up where according to convention they do not belong. But while not determining, probability is *telling*. Experienced birders come to respect and depend on it to help them formulate an identification, and test it, too.

Over time, I have come to regard *all* initial identifications not as conclusions but as hypotheses to be tested, initial best guesses. When I see a bird and quickly pin a name to it, what I am saying, in my mind, is: "I think it is a Lesser Yellowlegs. Now let's test this hypothesis to be sure." Let's study and see whether the traits I see conform to my initial identification.

One of the advantages of this approach is that you become less defensive about making a mistake. One of the other advantages is that you get to review the entire identification matrix, starting with the broad-brush hints and clues that prompted you to make your initial identification in the first place—habitat, size, shape, posture, behavior—and reconfirm it using whatever classic field marks might be evident.

Not only is this a good way to keep from making mistakes, it is a good way to sharpen your identification skills—if, in fact, your initial identification proves . . .

WRONG!

I love misidentifying birds, and I have had a lot of practice doing so. Over the course of my birding career, I'm sure I've been guilty of thousands of misidentifications, and that's just the ones I have caught myself or had pointed out to me.

But the reason I love misidentifications is because I learn more about bird identification when I am wrong than when I am right. Correct identifications are, after all, the expected norm—what commonly happens when a careful birder sees a bird well enough to note distinguishing traits.

But misidentifications are anomalous, exciting. The challenge for new and experienced birders alike becomes understanding what it was about the angle, distance, light, movement, or plumage that led you to believe a bird was another species entirely. You learn, at the very least, to respect the similarity between the two species you have just confused, and you hope that what you learn will keep you from making the same mistake again.

Misidentification does not end the game. Misidentification just resets the board for the next match.

How Identifications Go Wrong

Misidentifications evolve just as birders do. Beginning birders make fundamental mistakes—errors that are honest, easy to predict, and just as easy to correct. Experienced birders make errors from carelessness or misassessment or, believe it or not, experience itself.

Stage 1 Misidentification: Pinning the Cow to the Donkey. Early on, most misidentifications are rooted in basic inexperience. What beginners commonly do is see a bird. Note some eye-catching characteristics. Open a field guide. Stop at the first likeness. Jam the peg into the first likely hole.

It's how you turned the flicker into a thrush way back in the beginning of this book. But your misidentifications are more advanced now.

Stage 2 Misidentification: Pinning the Udder to the Donkey. Once birders gain experience, once they get the idea of family groupings sorted out, most misidentifications are caused by misassessing traits—most commonly size but also things like color, bill shape, and so on. A faulty perception of traits commonly leads to confusion between similar species.

Many years ago, during a World Series of Birding, I panned my scope along a lineup of Forster's Terns in breeding plumage. Among the ranks was one bird that towered over the rest and showed a bright orange bill and shaggy black crest.

"Royal Tern," I announced, and all my teammates agreed.

But upon closer inspection, the bird turned out to be just another Forster's Tern—one standing atop a mound of mud. Seen head-on, bill size was not apparent (only color), and a breeding-plumage Forster's has a full black crest almost as shaggy as a Royal's.

It was an understandable mistake, even an excusable mistake. But it was still a mistake, one rooted in a faulty initial assessment.

Stage 3 Misidentification: Pinning the Donkey to the Tail.
This one is a bit mystifying, and one that experienced birders are
prone to. Do you remember back in chapter 4 when I said that you
have just sown the seeds for one of the most common pitfalls in
bird identification? Well, here it is. The skill set that you have spent
so much time building not only makes it easier for you to identify
birds but to misidentify them, too. All your knowledge about
birds—their habits, habitat, movement patterns, distribution—predisposes you to anticipate them in certain places at certain times,
and then find them even when they are not there.

A small, brown bird jumps, and you get only a fleeting glimpse
of it. Your mind fills in the blank.

"House Wren!"

Chances are you were right. Probability says you were right and
supports what you saw. But what if the bird wasn't a House Wren?
What if it was in actual fact a Carolina Wren? What if it was a
Dunnock—a small wrenlike bird that has never been recorded in
North America?

Yet.

Either way, your identification is wrong.

Birds seen imperfectly are *never* truly identified. Unless confirmed by subsequent study, snap identifications are no better
than educated guesses. They are speculations, not identifications.
Build into your identification process a margin of error, and a little
humility.

Birds need not be seen fleetingly or imperfectly to be misidentified, however. Experience predisposes birders to anticipate certain
birds in certain places and causes them to overlook (a.k.a., misidentify) birds that are similar but less likely.

Several years ago, on a Christmas Bird Count, I and two other
experienced birders spent the last hour of the day scanning an area
of marsh. Near dusk, my gaze fell on a bird perched about seventy
yards away. Something about the shape and posture prompted me
to train a spotting scope on what proved to be a Northern Shrike. I
felt pretty smug about it until one of my companions pointed out,
somewhat sheepishly, that the bird had been sitting there for at
least fifteen minutes. All of us had passed our binoculars over it

multiple times, and all had dismissed it as a Northern Mockingbird, the expected light gray, high-perch-sitting, upright-postured passerine of our region.

But the most egregious errors rooted in experience are those in which skilled birders venture out, conscious of the fact that they are at a time and in a place where a very rare and desirable bird is possible—not likely, of course, but possible—and . . .

Ohmygodtheregoesonenow!

Under the influence of this poisonous blend of wisdom and wishful thinking, I have turned Virginia Rails into Black Rails, Great Blue Herons into Bald Eagles, even Clorox bottles into Snowy Owls.

You don't have to be an inexperienced birder to make egregious errors. In fact, it often helps to be a very experienced one.

OK, this is a real Snowy Owl. But put a mile or so between you and it and the bird's similarity to a beached Clorox bottle becomes manifest.

7 | A World of Sound: The Universe X2

We were standing on a grassy hilltop, somewhere in Sussex County, New Jersey, in the dark hour before dawn. It was during the World Series of Birding. My teammates and I were one of ninety teams scattered across the Garden State, bringing our bird-watching skills to bear. At the moment, our senses were trained on the sky above—a beautiful sky filled with stars and the disembodied call notes of migrating birds.

"Black-billed Cuckoo," five voices chimed as the rattling chortle of this shy bird of the forest understory settled to earth and was picked up by five sets of ears. Black-billed Cuckoo is a bird easily missed on a New Jersey "Big Day." Getting the bird by call, at night, is your best bet.

"An-another," whispered two of our team members whose hearing was particularly acute. Then another closer bird called. Another. Another. By the sixth or tenth call, nobody bothered to pin a name to the bird. But every additional cuckoo vocalization prompted chuckles and heads shaken in disbelief (which of course went unnoticed in the dark).

Some years we miss the bird. This year a veritable avalanche of Black-billed Cuckoos was migrating overhead. Of course, the birds were invisible. But the magnitude of the flight was no less spectacular and our appreciation was undiminished (in fact, it was enhanced by our pride in the reach of our skills).

Adding to the acoustic smorgasbord were the piping call notes of assorted warblers, the clear whistles and nasal yelps of thrushes, and the *seep* notes of sparrows. Each species heard and identified was one less species we'd have to track down in the daylight.

It was a perfect night for listening and a perfect example of why learning bird vocalizations is not just helpful but fundamental to birding.

Lag Time

It's a phrase so often uttered (and heard) that it amounts to a bird-watching cliché: "I'm a pretty good birder, but I still don't know bird calls."

Join the club. For many, perhaps most, birders, their last frontier is the audio frontier.

Maybe it's because we are, for the most part, a vision-driven species. Maybe it's because the term "bird watching" skews our focus. But I think, for many new birders, it's a simple matter of not giving proper regard to the advantage our ears accord us.

Birds live in a visual *and* auditory world. Our sensory abilities overlap theirs. Birding by sight and not sound is the avocational equivalent of hopping on one foot. Learn bird vocalizations and you have more than doubled the reach of your bird identification (and location) skills.

By recognizing the songs and call notes of birds, you'll identify birds faster. You'll identify birds with more confidence. And, as in the case just presented, you'll be able to identify birds when your visual skills are thwarted by conditions, distance, even darkness.

It's Hard, But It's Not

I know what you are thinking. You're wrong. You can do this. Anyone whose hearing is not impaired can.

Can you recognize the caw of a crow? The honk of a Canada Goose? Well the same auditory detection and recollection skills you use to identify these species apply to every other bird species on the planet.

There is another reason I know you can learn to recognize birds by their vocalizations. I know because I can do it. Not only do I

have lousy hearing but I too never really tried to gain a tympanic toehold in birding until I was years into my development.

I've spent most of my birding life playing catch up. Back in grammar school, I used to anticipate the day my classmates and I would be trundled off to the nurse's office to have our eyes and ears tested. My eyesight was fantastic, off the charts (literally). I'd sit down in the chair (with the cardboard square over one eye). The nurse would look up. Roll her eyes skyward. Go right down to the bottom line on the chart, which I could rattle off with ease.

I always thought it unfair that there weren't a couple of smaller sets of letters to challenge me.

But when she put the earphones over my head and started going through the tonal sequence, there were periods of silence (coinciding with her quizzical gaze) when I knew my left (or right) hand was supposed to be elevated—except no motor-triggering sound was reaching my ears.

Let me correct that. The sound was reaching my ears. But since my hearing is at the low end of normal for all frequencies and fifty percent deficient at four thousand hertz, I wasn't detecting it.

So there I was. A visual Einstein with Beethoven's hearing and nobody to tell me that in addition to looking at birds, I should be listening to them, too.

Like I'm telling you, now.

Matter of Course

The way to approach the challenge of learning bird vocalizations is to give it the same significance you accord identifying birds by sight. Vocalizations are as important, useful, and determining as any field mark. They are at least as important an element in the bird identification matrix as size, shape, plumage, behavior, and flight.

So why didn't I mention it until now? First, because from a tutorial perspective, the world of sound and the human auditory package are different enough from sight to warrant a separate discussion. Second, because for better or worse, we tend to be a visual-centric species. For most people, a bird vocalization is just a disembodied sound.

If I'm walking with you, a Western Meadowlark flies in front of us, and I say, "there's a Western Meadowlark," you will automatically link the name and the bird. If we're walking along, a Western Meadowlark sings, and I say, "there's a Western Meadowlark," you are very probably going to say, "Huh?" The bird's song never crossed the threshold of your awareness.

I've met hundreds of people who have told me that they "got into birding because they saw this bird in their yard." I don't recall a single person ever telling me that they got into birding because they *heard* this bird in their yard.

So the reason this book began with a visual focus was to fall in accord with the human predilection, in fact, the cognitive addiction, to visual stimulus. For most people, it is easier to ascribe a bird's song to a bird they know than to pin the image of a bird to a song they heard.

Some people, of course, are very auditorially attuned. Birders who are visually impaired thrive in an acoustical universe—they analyze, sort, and lock away sounds in a fashion that visually fixated birders can only envy. Birding by ear is just as challenging as birding by sight. It is as emotionally gratifying. It is just as bonding.

But most birders, most humans, in fact, find it useful to have a visual anchor on which to pin a vocalization—an image to link to a sound.

OK, you see the bird. You've got your anchorage. Time to stop birding on one foot and move your auditory foot forward.

Songs vs. Calls

For the most part, bird vocalizations are broken down into two broad categories: bird songs and bird calls. Songs, most commonly vocalized by male birds, and, most commonly, by male birds on their breeding territories, tend to be more complex utterances. Calls are usually short, often one or two notes, given by both sexes throughout the year. Where most species have a single song or song type, that same species will have a variety of calls, different calls conveying different information.

Some calls are used as a warning. Some to solicit food. Some to simply say, "I am here."

Though more complex, songs are in many ways easier to learn than calls. Their multiple elements (notes, pitch, cadence, rhythm,

If we're walking along, a Western Meadowlark vocalizes, and I say "there's a Western Meadowlark," you are probably not going to connect the remark to the sound.

tone, and, especially, pattern) help distinguish them. Calls seem to fall into two classes: easy to learn and hard.

Recognizing the screeching bray of scrub jay or the cluck of a hen turkey is easy. Distinguishing the subtle difference between the nocturnal flight call of Yellow Warbler and Northern Waterthrush is more challenging.

Oh Say Can You Hear?

One way to approach the challenge of learning bird vocalizations is the same way you approached bird recognition. By starting with the vocalizations you already know.

We've established that you know the loud, harsh *caw* of American Crow and the bugled, two-note *ah-honk* of Canada Goose. Maybe you are familiar with the roosterlike crow of a Ring-necked Pheasant, the quack of a Mallard, the keening cry of a Herring Gull, or the croaking rattle of a Sandhill Crane.

The croaking rattle of Sandhill Crane may not be as familiar to most people as the coo of a pigeon or the quack of a Mallard, but it is just as distinctive and as easily committed to memory.

How about the coo of a pigeon? The bray of a Blue Jay? If you live in the South, you likely wake most mornings to the musical *(ta) too, too, too, too, too, too, too, too* of the Northern Cardinal. If you are in northern lake country, the yodeled laughter of the Common Loon is part of your audio repertoire. If you live almost anywhere in North America, you have heard the song of the American Robin: a rich, cheery, run-on ensemble of mostly two-note phrases that go up and down the scale.

You don't know the robin's song? No, you probably don't. But you really should. If you learn American Robin, then you are not far from knowing the song of the Scarlet Tanager, a song that is like American Robin's in pattern, but the notes are hoarser, more slurred, and given with a slower, lazier cadence. And if you know the song of a Scarlet Tanager, you'll note, when you hear your first Yellow-throated Vireo, that the two-note phrases have a similar hoarse, slurred quality—but instead of being run-on, like the robin's and tanager's, the vireo pauses between phrases.

That's right: Just as in birding by sight, vocalizations give you a foundation that allows you to compare, contrast, and broaden the scope of the auditory net you cast at the world.

If you know the harsh *caw, caw, caw* of the American Crow, you'll discover that the smaller Fish Crow sounds like an American Crow with a cold.

If you know the two-note bugle of Canada Goose, then when you hear the higher-pitched, more compressed, more single-noted yelp of Snow Goose, your ears should register the difference.

The quack of Mallard? Gadwall, another puddle duck, has a quack that is similar but more muffled, and more nasal. And ducks are not the only birds that quack. Least Bittern, a small, butterscotch-colored heron that skulks among marsh reeds, has a call that sounds like a rapid, descending, three-note quack.

It also gives a hurried series of muffled, gulping coos. Like pigeon? No, more like Black-billed Cuckoo. But Black-billed Cuckoos don't call from reed beds.

Every vocalization you learn is not only another piece in the auditory puzzle, it is the comparative foundation for the next piece.

So I'll Have to Say I Love You in a Song

Apologies to Jim Croche, but one of the primary functions of bird-song is to attract a mate. To a consenting female, the song of American Robin translates as: "Hi, my name is Mr. Right."

The other reason males vocalize is to sing rings around their territory. To other males, the translation goes: "Listen, bub, this territory is mine and yours is somewhere else."

From the standpoint of identifying birds, learning song is arguably less valuable and more limited than learning calls. In the Northern Hemisphere, most species sing only during the breeding season—March through July.

But when birds are on their breeding ground, males are vocal precisely because they want to be heard. This makes them easy to find. And this is precisely why learning how to recognize birds by their vocalizations is so important.

The world of sound is more pervasive and engaging than the restricted slice of universe granted by our eyes. Our sight is restricted by degrees of arc (i.e., more than half of what goes on in the universe does so behind your back) and by darkness. Sound vaults distance, passes through visual barriers (such as trees), and can be detected no matter which way we're facing.

Bird calls are often more muted and subtle, directed at birds of the same species or mates or members of a flock or family group. When birds sing, they sing to the universe.

The Hills (and Marshes, and Prairies, and Deserts, and Mountains, and Valleys) are Alive with the Sound of Birdsong

There are few people on the planet who can hear a bird sing once and commit the song to memory. If you are one of them, then chances are you are also a professional musician, one whose mind is already trained to register, analyze, and package sound.

We audio duffers face a tougher challenge—the first of which is to train ourselves to hear bird vocalizations at all. This is harder than you think. Even before leaving the crib, your ears have been picking up bird sounds, but your brain has been trained to ignore them, treating bird vocalizations the way your email treats spam.

You are going to have to reprogram yourself to be attuned to bird sounds. Once you do, your life will never be the same.

When you stand next to a skilled field birder, you are standing next to a sensory sponge. The two of you may be talking about the merits of the latest field guide or a good place to get a sandwich, but the ears, and a portion of the mind, of your keen birding friend are filtering the world of sound, isolating and analyzing bird vocalizations.

The vocalizations of common species may elicit no conscious response—the brain may simply relegate them to the "common and expected" category. But a vocalization of an unusual or desirable species will kick a bird brain to a higher level of awareness, and may even prompt a conversation-trumping response.

"Upland Sandpiper!"

"You want Upland Sandpiper on your sandwich?"

"No, it just called. Somewhere overhead."

No matter how poor your ears are at detecting bird sounds, your brain can still be trained to be more attentive to them. It's a matter of focus and practice, and this means spending as much time as possible in the field, listening as intently as you are watching.

Song Paralysis

If you listen to a bird's song with the vague ambition of simply "learning it" or "recognizing it," you are going to find that your mind is not very good at filing away this sort of disembodied information.

This is another way of saying that most of us are not born with the audio-recall of an Igor Stravinski.

I have a friend, an enthusiastic but casual birder named Jay, who once accompanied me on a Christmas Bird Count. In winter, in New Jersey, very few birds sing full songs. Call, yes. Sing, no. But one of those birds (in fact, just about the only winter vocalist) is the Carolina Wren, a bird that maintains not only its territory but its mate year-round. Carolina Wren is also a persistent vocalist, singing all day.

So all morning, as we birded along, Carolina Wrens were sounding off, singing loud, ringing renditions of their classic *teakettle, teakettle, teakettle* song.

And every time a wren sang, Jay would ask, "Pete, what's that one?"

And every time, I'd reply, "Carolina Wren."

Over the course of the morning, we probably had this dialogue six or nine times.

After lunch, in fact, almost as soon as we vacated the car, we were greeted by a loud, ringing *teakettle, teakettle, teakettle, teakettle.*

And Jay asked, "Pete, what's that one?"

And instead of answering, I pointed a finger at Jay, who, after a moment's hesitation, offered, "Carolina Wren?"

For the rest of the afternoon, every time a wren vocalized, Jay would ask, and I would point. And he would reply, "Carolina Wren?"

He was right every time. But he also went through the entire day hearing, but never actually recognizing, much less retaining, the song of a Carolina Wren.

Listen to It. Liken It. Label It.

Remember how we approached the challenge of identifying birds by sight? The step-down process that first places birds in their proper family section and then row and then seat? Birdsong can be approached in the same way—but with one major difference.

You are not always, or necessarily ever, going to be grouping bird songs into "family groups." Not all warblers "warble." You are going to be grouping songs into categories based on the pattern of the bird's song.

There are several basic song pattern types. Recognize them, and you begin the process of hearing birdsong critically. You also start a bundling and sorting process that helps you liken the bird you are hearing to one group of singers, thus distinguishing it from others. Finally, you have the latitude to categorize and compare any new song you are hearing with the fundamentally similar songs that you are already familiar with—songs that are similar in pattern but differ in terms of volume, pitch, tonal quality, speed of delivery . . .

Sound subtle? Yes, it can be. That's why the sorting system is based on song pattern. It's fundamental.

Basic Song Types: The First Major Cut

I tend to group songs into five basic song types: Run-on Repeater, Trill, Simple Two- and Three-Part Songs, Perpetual Change-up songs, and Complex Songs.

Run-on Repeater. The easiest song group to recognize is the Run-on Repeater—songs that employ a single note or phrase and repeat it start to finish. It is one of the most common song types. In this category, you will find the songbirds already mentioned:

Northern Cardinal, whose loud, whistled *too, too, too, too, too, too, too, too, too* song resonates across the eastern two-thirds of the country as well as southeastern Canada and the American Southwest.

Carolina Wren, whose repeated *teakettle, teakettle, teakettle* phrase is more complex than the cardinal's but no less repetitive.

Other birds that fall into this category include a small warbler, Common Yellowthroat, whose *witchity, witchity, witchity* song is a common feature of freshwater marshes, weedy fields, and open woodland understory. And Northern (and Gilded) Flicker, whose loud *wicKa, wicKa, wicKa* sounds like a run-on series of musical hiccups.

In the East, many people are familiar with the nocturnal call of Whip-poor-will. Across much of the West, the nocturnal serenade of *poor-will, poor-will, poor-will* is just as familiar.

Sometimes these repetitive singers will sing the same note or phrase for a time, then switch to different phrases. This is one of the signature characteristics of the song of Hutton's Vireo, a tiny bird of the West Coast and southwestern oak forests.

Sometimes the notes quicken or become more compressed or grow louder or softer as the song draws to an end. The song of the Cactus Wren, often likened to the sound of an old car starting, begins slow and accelerates: *rah, rah, rah, rahrahrahrahrah.* (Northern

The Northern Cardinal's song is a simple series of repeated notes. Sometimes it remains true to the pattern start to finish; sometimes it is two parted.

Cardinal will sometimes do the same thing: *too, too, too, too-too-too-too-too-too-too.*)

Trill. A common and distinctive song type, but also one that can be hard to differentiate. In one sense, it is like the Run-on Repeater. It consists, basically, of a single note. The difference is that the notes are so rapid and compressed that they blend into a chatter or trill.

Some trillers, such as the Dark-eyed Junco, have a short, slow, musical trill; Swamp Sparrow has a rich, musical trill that is border-line warble. Some, such as the Chipping Sparrow's, are faster, with notes that are more clipped and mechanical. The trill of the Worm-eating Warbler is rapid, almost a blur, and brittle sounding.

Telling trilling species apart is greatly aided by habitat. A trilling bird in a cattail swamp in Quebec is very probably a Swamp Sparrow. The forest-dwelling Dark-eyed Junco is eliminated by habitat. The Worm-eating Warbler, a bird of brushy woodland understory, is likewise eliminated by habitat (and range).

But the differences between trilling species are often qualitative. With practice, you'll note that some species will sound drier or breathier or clipped or more musical or . . .

You can just track down the singer and get visual confirmation—that what you are dealing with is a warbler, or a sparrow that trills. That alone helps narrow down the possibilities, since not all warblers or sparrows are trillers.

Simple Two- and Three-Part Songs. Many birds' songs have separate parts—very commonly an opening sequence followed by a distinctly different second half. Songs with three distinct parts not uncommon, but two-parted songs are most common. Songs like White-throated Sparrow's *Ohhhh, say, say, say, say, say.* Or Nashville Warbler's *Seebit, seebit, seebit. Seebit, see, see, see, see, see.* By comparison, the song of the Tennessee Warbler is sharper, more hurried, and three parted: *chi, chi, chi, chi, chi churchurchurchrch'h'h'h'h'h'h.*

There are also songs that involve multiple changing phrases but generally remain loyal to a pattern of delivery.

Perpetual Change-up Songs. Where some birds sing short sets with a break in between, others sing on and on and on, but their songs consist of an ever-changing series of one-, two-, or three-note phrases.

A prime example is the Red-eyed Vireo, a forest bird whose song is a rambling, ongoing (in fact, never-ending) series of simple two- and three-note whistled phrases, each slightly different and separated by a short pause. Compare this to the Yellow-breasted Chat, whose song is an ongoing series of somewhat comical toots, whistles, gargles, and chatters (with a savoring pause between each single- or multiple-note set), or Curve-billed Thrasher, whose song is a nonstop, run-on series of mostly two-note phrases (how the bird breathes remains a mystery).

Complex Songs. Some birds' songs involve multiple elements, notes that change in pitch, pattern, volume, and delivery (as well as complexity). On the simple end of the scale is the song of the American Robin, whose song is a run-on, shifting series of whistled two- and three-note phrases that swing up, and down, and up, and down—punctuated by a savoring pause and, perhaps, a few bleating clucks. Then it's on to another set.

The House Wren's song is harder to describe. It's a loud, hurried, rambling series of warbles, musical chatters, and trills that seems to rise to a crescendo. Just as complex is the song of the Ruby-crowned Kinglet, a surprisingly loud, mostly high-pitched, and protracted jumble of notes that begins with several high, clear warm-up notes before degenerating into a rapid, rambling tirade that often includes, somewhere in the sequence, a few high, clear, chickadeelike *dee, dee, dee*s. These songs might be difficult to describe and render. But they are usually consistent in their quality and complexity and broad pattern of delivery.

Often, too, there are individual notes or elements in these more complex songs that the memory can fix upon. The pattern-breaking, chickadeelike *dee, dee, dee* notes in the kinglet's song. Or, in the case of Canada Warbler, a bird whose short, loud, hurried jumble of clear, whistled notes is almost always preceded by a single introductory *chip*.

Opening and closing notes are often the key to teflon-coated songs, songs that don't stick well in your memory. The White-eyed Vireo, for example, has a short song with a variable pattern, but it begins and usually ends with a distinctive, spitting *chip* note.

Putting the Song to Words

A tried-and-true technique for learning bird songs is to render them phonetically into words—mnemonics that replicate the rhythm and pattern of a bird's song in your mind. Some of have already been introduced to you: The "teakettle, teakettle, teakettle" song of Carolina Wren, for instance. One of my favorite phonetic translations relates to the bird just mentioned, White-eyed Vireo, whose song has been rendered as: "[spit] and see if I care [spit]." A cousin, the Warbling Vireo, has a song that is hurried and run-on, compressed, with the last note emphasized and rising. Some transcribe it as: "If I see it I can seize it and I'll squeeze it till it SquiRRTS."

But sometimes the words won't come, and when that happens, it might be possible to liken or link the songs of birds to some other clue. The song of Indigo Bunting has often been rendered as: "What what? Where where? Here here. See it! See it!" But in this species, song quality as much as pattern is what registers in my mind. The clear, whistled notes of this bunting's song seem "sharp and glittery" to me. When I hear it, the image of broken glass in sunlight flashes.

I may be the only person in the world who has this mental link—Indigo Bunting and broken glass—but it works for me. The trick is finding the tricks that work for you.

Bird Calls

Bird songs are useful and gratifying, but they are also limited. Limited, for the most part, to adult male birds. Limited to that relatively brief period in a bird's annual cycle when it is breeding. Bird calls are different. Birds call every day, all year round, and these vocalizations not only alert birders to the presence and location of birds but, to those familiar with bird calls, their identity.

Offered the choice between losing my ability to identify birds by sight or by call, I would ask for a time-out to consider my options. As gratifying as seeing birds is, I probably identify most birds by call, and I use bird calls not only to certify identifications but jumpstart them, too.

Take Greater and Lesser Yellowlegs, two long-legged shorebirds. Similar in structure and nearly identical in their plumage

White-eyed Vireo's song is short, sassy, and phonetically rendered as [spit] and see if I care [spit].

characteristics, the two species are nevertheless easily distinguished by call. Greater Yellowlegs' call is loud and ringing. Lesser Yellowlegs' is softer, more mellow.

Take Alder and Willow Flycatchers, two small birds of brushy edge that are notoriously difficult to separate in the field by structure and plumage but easily separated by songs and call.

Alder Flycatcher's song is a rough, three-noted *fee-Bee-o*. Willow's is a two-noted sneeze: *Fitz-bew*.

Alder's call is a flat *pip*. Willow's call a liquid *whit*.

Yes, it has taken a lifetime to gain this audio advantage. But I started knowing no more than you know now.

I recognized the call (or caw) of a crow. I recognized the honk of a Canada Goose. I recognized the hoot of a Great Horned Owl.

Many bird calls are just as easily learned as the American Crow's and Canada Goose's. Calls that are loud, distinctive, and commonly heard. The yodel of a Common Loon. The croaking rattle of Sandhill Crane. The namesake call of Greater Kiskadee.

And what does that sound like?

It sounds just like this large South Texas flycatcher's name. *Kis-ka-Dee*. In fact, the names of many birds are phonetic renderings of their calls (or songs). Examples: Eastern Wood *(Pee-oo-Ee)* Pewee, Common *(pur-RAH-kee)* Pauraque, *Whip-poor-will,* Blue *Jay, Chick-a-dee,* Eastern *(Toe-hee)* Towhee, *Kill-dee'r.*

Hardest to learn are the single-note utterances known as "flight calls." Difficult because many of these vocalizations are terse and, to human ears, similar in quality and delivery.

So how does someone go about gaining proficiency in the world of bird sound?

Easy. As you watch, you listen.

Then you watch and listen some more.

Focused Field Time: Drink This In

Even more than visual bird identification, learning the songs and calls of birds is something best done in the field. Yes, there are a number of aids: CDs that play the recorded songs and calls of birds and some that not only break down and analyze the elements of the vocalizations but also depict the sound, visually, in a diagrammatic sketch called a sonogram.

There are also apps that allow birders to scroll to species and call up the songs and calls in the field.

Bird recordings are helpful. Helpful for prep. Helpful for review or to help confirm (or deny) an identification. But as helpful as these aids are, there is nothing more helpful or rewarding than going into the field and using field time to not only study birds but listen to them, too.

In other words, there is nothing that beats real. Real birds, in real time, bill open, sound coming out. You see it. You hear it. You get it.

And given repeated exposure, you learn it. Given a growing body of songs and calls, you'll find it easier and easier to compare and contrast, liken and differentiate, distinguish and . . .

In time, even the very subtle differences between the individual call notes of birds become intelligible, the differences discernible to ears trained to hear them.

You start with the easy ones. The dry, emphatic *chack* of Red-winged Blackbird vs. the low, throaty *churk* of Western Meadowlark. The spring-peeper-like *heep* of a Swainson's Thrush flight call vs. the nasal, descending *veeer* flight call of the Veery.

Calls can often be likened to sounds you are already familiar with. The high, thin, breathy "sigh" of Cedar Waxwing reminds me of the "sighing" sound of a screen door closing. The *bink* flight call of Bobolink recalls to my ear distant, ceramic wind chimes sounding in the heavens. The croaking call of Sandhill Crane sounds like a gate set on ungreased, wooden hinges being closed.

Your ears will gradually grow more attuned to the elements and subtleties of sounds—volume, pitch, duration. Some chips have a rising inflection. Some descend. Some are sharp and emphatic beginning to end. Some are more muffled or drag at the beginning. Some are rich and full; some terse, spitting.

Don't just listen to the sound and try and remember it. Analyze it. Dissect it. Compare it to calls you already know. Liken it, encapsulate it in words.

Think of bird calls as you might a fine chardonnay. There was a time in your life when wine was wine. Then came white wine and red wine. Then came riesling (sweet), and pinot grigio (dry), and chardonnay, which is oaky, or peachy, or buttery, or tart, or tinged with apple, or . . .

Why, just the other night, I had a particularly fine Central Coast chardonnay with a buttery, rich texture and a complex, full-bodied blend of apple and apricot bounded by a subtle suggestion of oak that . . .

You don't drink? Oh. Well, just the other day, I was savoring the call note of a particularly fine Kentucky Warbler. It was loud, rich, low pitched, and full bodied, with a distinctly emphatic quality and just a suggestion of . . .

Here's (or maybe hear's) to your audio-birding success.
Cheers!

8 | After the Fundamentals: "Something Good"

I was twenty-four, a dedicated birder, and, by the time I discovered hawk watching, pretty confident that I was a competent birder—in fact, I was the best birder I knew. There was a reason for this. I didn't know any other birders.

Yet.

Through trial and error, I'd mastered the "confusing fall warblers." Felt reasonably comfortable pinning names to sparrows (in fact, in the Yukon, I had even correctly deduced that a bird I studied for two weeks was an out-of-range Clay-colored Sparrow [my first], not the expected Brewer's (Timberline) Sparrow [which would also have been a first]).

But hawks were my new challenge, and my passion led me to a place called Raccoon Ridge, a famous North Jersey hawk-watching junction. I found out about the place and got directions from a book. The guy I met up there, a retired teamster named Floyd Wolfarth, got directions from the man who discovered it, a fellow member of the North Jersey–based Urner Ornithological Club. He, and other club members, had been coming to Coon for more than forty years.

We exchanged greetings. Shared our sightings—which were, for the September date, pretty much in accord. Mostly Broad-winged Hawks with the odd Osprey and Sharp-shinned Hawk and American Kestrel thrown in. Then we both settled in to scanning the horizon for migrating birds of prey.

Finding distant hawks was something I was good at. So I was surprised when my new acquaintance announced: "I've got a bird. Just over Stiggs."

I didn't know the topographic reference point, but I did find the bird. Waaaay out there. A raptorial speck, riding the updraft of the ridge. It was on the flight path most birds had followed during the day, and most of these had been Broad-wings. To my undiscerning eyes, this bird looked little different.

Wrong again.

"Watch this bird!" Floyd rumbled. "Watch this bird! This is going to be something good!"

"How the heck can he tell that this isn't just another Broad-winged Hawk?" I wondered dismissively. But there was no missing the excitement in the man's voice, the anticipation. And as the bird drew closer, I had to admit that it really didn't look like the Broad-wings I'd been seeing. It was bigger, rangier . . . and, what was worse, I didn't have any idea what it was. Couldn't even put it into a category, a family: buteo, accipiter, falcon.

The bird came on. Passed just below eye level, offering an excellent view. But having neither the discipline to look critically at hawks in flight nor an understanding of what to look for, I did little more than stare as the bird went by. I had an image in my mind all right, but I didn't have a match indexed in my memory. I had, as I had gotten to be a better birder, grown accustomed to recognizing birds and stale at identifying them.

"Well?" said the veteran hawk-watcher, putting my skills to the test.

"Broad-wing?" I suggested, playing the probability card, knowing it was wrong.

Floyd looked disgusted. "Goshawk!" he said. *"Un-mis-takeable,"* he pronounced.

"A goshawk," I thought, replaying the memory of the juvenile bird in my mind, recognizing the correctness of the identification. Knowing too that without Floyd's help, I'd never have been able to identify it on my own.

My very first Northern Goshawk.

But most astonishing was Floyd's ability to recognize things about this bird at distances that were not only beyond my skill, but beyond my imagination. I had no idea that anybody could look at a bird more than a mile away and suspect, perhaps even know, that it was something not just different but special.

Until that day. The day I discovered that bird watching's tribal skill level was leagues ahead of my own. If pushing the identification horizon was where I wanted my skill level to be, then it was time for me to start learning from the wisdom of the tribe.

Solo vs. Tribal

Birding can be a solitary or a social endeavor. For many, it is both. While there is no right or wrong way to go birding, there is an easy and a hard way. If you go birding solely by yourself, you are going to experience more frustration than you would by availing yourself of the wisdom of more experienced birders.

Experienced birders know where to go and when in order to see the greatest concentrations of birds. They understand how seasons and weather affect bird distribution. They know tricks and short-cuts that get quickly to identifications, hints and clues that have not even been included in field guides . . .

Best of all, they can correct you when you misidentify a bird and guide you to the right identification. You can learn to identify birds through trial and error. But uncorrected errors set you back, and the confidence instilled by someone confirming an identification moves you forward.

Meeting Floyd was one of the luckiest breaks in my life. For the next year, I had what amounted to a private birding tutor. From this celebrated member of the New Jersey birding community, I learned what would have taken me a lifetime to glean on my own.

You don't have to wait for a lucky encounter. There are hundreds of institutions and events all across North America dedicated to bringing new birders to greater skill levels: local bird clubs, state Audubon offices and societies, national birding organizations, introduction to birding courses, regularly scheduled bird walks, birding festivals, birding tours, birding camps, and birding sites whose objective is to instill skills and impart wisdom (and save you frustration).

If you are serious about becoming a better birder, you are best served by going out with birders more experienced than you are now.

No matter how much you enjoy your private time, if you are serious about learning how to identify birds, it is important to take advantage of the skills of birders who are more experienced.

That being said, to earn your birding wings, you need to go solo, too.

Bobble-Head Birders

I know people who have birded thirty and forty years who cannot tell a Savannah Sparrow from a Song Sparrow or a female Green-winged Teal from a Blue-winged. Because they've never seen them? Actually, no. They've seen hundreds. But they have never identified them. They never had to. They fell into the habit, early on, of birding with a group and letting the leader and the more experienced birders identify the birds for them.

Is this a bad thing? Not necessarily. If your ambition is to go afield with friends and see different birds, this is a perfectly fine way to go birding. But if your objective is to build and improve your *own* identification skills, then being a bobble-head birder—one

I know people who have birded for thirty years and still cannot tell a Savannah Sparrow (like this one) from a Song Sparrow. Because they never saw one? No. Because they never tried to identify one all by themselves.

whose contribution to every identification challenge is to offer an affirmative nod—then you have sold yourself and your ambition short.

Yes, you absolutely should go out with more experienced birders. Take advantage of their skills. Learn their tricks and techniques. Discover where bird identification's horizon lies.

But to make those skills your own, you must apply them on your own. Challenge and push yourself. Suffer the frustration but savor the gratification of making your own identifications.

The only person who can advance your personal skill set is you. Lots of people can identify a bird for you. It's up to you to take the initiative and take identification to the next level. This is recognition. The ability to know birds at a glance because, through study and trial and error, you have gained a familiarity with the species.

The tendency to coast along when in the company of more accomplished birders is not unique to beginners (or perennial neophytes). In the World Series of Birding, there is a strong temptation for team members to slack off toward the end of the day and let the best birder in the group, or the team member assigned to scout the area, carry the ID load.

My wife, Linda, who is an exceptionally skilled birder, admits that when she and I bird together at home in New Jersey, she has a tendency to let me find the birds. Because I'm a better birder? No, because when we were first married, my home-turf experience was superior, and she got into the habit, early on, of letting me lead.

When the two of us are birding in the tropics, our roles are reversed. Because of her skill, and because she takes pains to familiarize herself with the species we may encounter on a trip, it is Linda who is the superior birder, finding and identifying most of the birds, and me who goes along for the ride.

So absolutely, yes, go birding with a group. But to become the skilled field birder you want to be, it is essential that you go out on your own, too.

The Holistic Challenge

When David Sibley, Clay Sutton, and I wrote *Hawks in Flight*, it was heralded as a breakthrough. It wasn't. It was just the codification of a natural advance of skills, an advanced form of field identification

that you are now eminently positioned to transition into. If you have taken to heart the holistic approach to bird identification promoted in this book, then you are versed in an identification process that will permit you to identify birds as far away as you can perceive them.

It's people who are indentured to a system of bird identification that is dependent on classic field marks who are daunted by distance. But by becoming familiar with, and comfortable with, the behavioral hints and clues that are part of the identification matrix, you are able to pin names to birds at distances where plumage, and even structural characteristics, are indiscernible.

You did this by studying every new bird you found. You did this by embracing, early on, an identification technique that incorporated *all* the hints and clues a bird was throwing at you.

Take sandpipers and plovers. Plovers forage by walking and stopping (like American Robins): Walk. Stop. Pick. Walk. Stop. Walk. Stop. Pick. Sandpipers feed on the run, advancing and picking or probing at the same time.

At half a mile, you can tell feeding sandpipers and plovers apart by noting nothing more than how they feed. You don't need to get close enough to note the different bill shapes (short and blunt for plovers, pointy for sandpipers).

It's a starting point. A differentiating first cut. Shorebirds constitute one of the most challenging bird groups to identify. But with one bold, behavior-based stroke, you have simplified the challenge–divided the group in half.

OK, by one-quarter and three-quarters (there are more sandpipers than plovers).

What do you say we continue down this path? Let's confront a hypothetical challenge, you and me, and put this holistic birding approach to the test. Let's pretend we are birding a stretch of mid-Atlantic beach in early September. The beach is overrun with migrating shorebirds, some near, most far. By September, the ranks of shorebirds are filled with juvenile birds, and adults have, for the most part, already molted out of their more colorful breeding plumage.

Looking at the birds closest to us, it is apparent that one species of sandpiper is numerically dominant. A fist-sized shorebird bunched in tight groups that races up and down the beach, pursuing and being pursued by the retreating and advancing waves. They're overall pale, almost whitish, with pale gray upper parts and bright white underparts. Looking close, you see blackish smudges on their shoulders.

Everything about this bird—its size, plumage, feeding behavior, habitat—says Sanderling, a common, small, hyperactive sandpiper specialized to feed in the wave zone of high-energy, sandy beaches. Most sandpipers prefer to feed on mudflats or in shallow, standing water. Sanderling, just as the name implies, are partial to sand—in fact, are almost never found on mud. The bird's scientific name, *Calidris alba,* underscores another trait that is easily noted and supports the identification. *Calidris alba. Alba.* Latin for *white.* So a white(ish) *Calidris* sandpiper. In nonbreeding plumage, most of the other sandpipers in this genus are conspicuously grayer or browner backed than Sanderling, a distinction that is, of course, most apparent in direct comparison.

Which is where we are going next, and where the advantage of having a comparative bellwether bird like Sanderling now becomes apparent.

Just above the reach of the waves is a less energetic shorebird that is feeding like a plover: walk, stop, pick. There are several of these birds, fairly widely spaced, and about the same size as Sanderling. They are also distinctly darker backed than Sanderling.

You've just defined Semipalmated Plovers. Black-bellied Plovers and Golden-Plovers would be much larger than Sanderlings. Piping Plovers as pale as Sanderling. It's the wrong habitat for Killdeer (which are also conspicuously larger than Sanderlings), and Wilson's Plover and Snowy Plover would be out of range, so the possibility of seeing several individuals would be remote.

The birds were too far away to note the single, dark breast band. And you couldn't see a touch of orange at the base of the bill. But the bird is no less a Semipalmated Plover.

Moving on, you are aware that shorebirds are gregarious, and that mixed-species flocks are typical. Accordingly, you scan through the Sanderling flock—not looking for any particular species but for anything anomalous to catch your eye. A larger bird or smaller bird or darker bird (since our baseline species is Sanderling, there really are no paler possibilities).

Semipalmated Plover and Semipalmated Sandpiper, representing two different shorebird families with two distinctly different feeding behaviors. Plovers walk. Stop. Pick. . . . Walk. Stop. Pick. Sandpipers feed on the run.

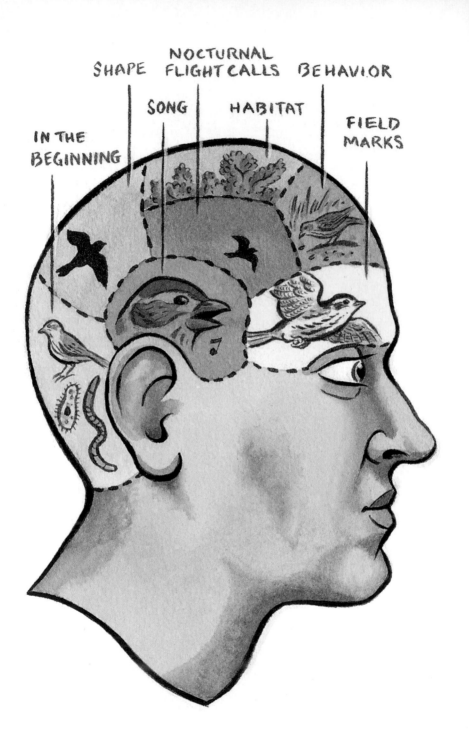

Graduation day, reader. It's the Delaware Bay in late May. The substrate is sand. There are five species of sandpiper here. Based on plumage and relative size (and date and distribution), your job is to find and identify them. Three is a passing grade.

Sure enough, mixed in with the ranks of Sanderling is a conspicuously larger, slightly darker, and overall grayer shorebird shaped much like a big, beefy Sanderling. The only Atlantic Coast sandpiper that meets this description is Red Knot.

Also amid the Sanderling are several slightly browner-backed sandpipers of about the same size. Most other *Calidris* sandpipers are smaller than Sanderling. Of the three *Calidris* sandpipers that are about the same size as Sanderling, Pectoral Sandpiper absolutely shuns sandy beach, and Purple Sandpiper is almost never found foraging on anything but rocks. This leaves Dunlin, a droop-billed sandpiper with "dun"-colored upperparts that is at home on beaches as well as mudflats and very commonly feeds with Sanderling.

Maybe it's wrong to say that we "identified" Semipalmated Plover, Red Knot, and Dunlin using a holistic approach. It's more nearly correct to say that we deduced the identity of these species using a combination of habitat, behavior, comparative size, distribution, and range.

In the final analysis, birds are not identified by the eyes. They are not identified with the ears. They are identified with the mind. The more information you can feed this identification factory, the farther your skills will reach and the more certainty you will be able to apply to your identification.

It begins with habitat. It moves on to placing birds in their proper groups and paring away other possibilities. It incorporates all the hints and clues that you amass through your study of birds in the field—from fine points of plumage to behavioral characteristics to direct comparison with proximal species. It demands that you test your hypothesis, your initial identification, applying the elements that determine probability.

It leads to a skill set that grows as your experience does, and that you can bring to bear upon birds no matter how far away they are.

9 | When Birds Cheat: Exceptions to the Rule

lied. Way back in the beginning of this book, I took some liberty with a fundamental truism. I told you that "what a bird is, and what it looks like, are one." It's time to admit that sometimes this is not the case.

I know, I know, I know. Hear me out.

Yes, this principle is fundamental to bird identification. Calling it into question undermines not only confidence but the whole concept of field identification. I'm going to amend the creed, not abolish it. I'm going to tell you, now, that there are certain exceptions to the rule. Times and conditions when species look, in actual fact or appearance, not as they are supposed to.

Things that alter a bird's physical appearance include molt, staining, physical deformity, and hybridization with similar species. Add to these real physical aberrations changes in appearance caused by light conditions, angle, and weather.

Take molt. At some point, birds are obligated to shed their old, used feathers and replace them with new ones. Some species do this piecemeal, over the course of many months. Some species undergo the process in a compressed time period going on several weeks. In both cases, the plumage (and the appearance of the bird) is altered.

For example, in June, most second-year Broad-winged Hawks are molting outer flight feathers, leaving a gap near the tip of the open wing that resembles a pale "crescent window," a characteristic of the similar Red-shouldered Hawk. In late summer, Red-winged

Blackbirds are often tail-less (radically altering their shape), and at all times of year it is possible to encounter other species so terminally truncated—perhaps a Mourning Dove or junco whose tail feathers were last seen in the talons of a hunting Sharp-shinned or Cooper's Hawk.

Molting male ducks may show little (if any) of the traits that make them so easy to recognize in full, fresh plumage. A cardinal infested with feather lice may be crestless (in fact, entirely bald). Simple wear and aging make plumage less vibrant over time, and signature characteristics, such as the broad, white terminal band on the tail of a Cooper's Hawk, may be worn thin, even broomed away.

Plumages can also be discolored or stained by birds feeding on berries or foraging in iron- or tannin-rich water or coming into contact with man-made agents like tar or oil. There was one very famous example of a long-legged shorebird at Brigantine National Wildlife Refuge in New Jersey that was initially identified as a Spotted Redshank, a European species, but proved to be just an oil-stained Greater Yellowlegs. Know too that ornithologists often "mark" birds they are studying with dye (typically orange, yellow, or blue) to make them easy to spot in the field.

But there are times when molt can also be an advantage. Semipalmated and Western Sandpipers are very similar—differing in structure and plumage by fine degrees. But from late July to late August, it is easy to tell adult birds apart. Western Sandpipers, which winter primarily in North America, are in heavy molt and have missing flight feathers. Semipalmated Sandpipers, which winter in South America, don't molt their flight feathers until they reach their wintering grounds. So before September, an adult Western-or-Semipalmated Sandpiper showing gaps in the wing is going to be a Western.

Hybrid progeny of two different species can show the traits of both parents, and while hybridization is rare in many species, it is common in others. Gulls and waterfowl commonly interbreed (not, of course, with each other!). Typical hybrids include Glaucous-winged x Western Gull and Mallard x Pintail.

Actually, male Mallards seem particularly randy and open-minded about partners. Mallard x domestic duck hybrids are common wherever duck ponds are found.

One of the most remarkable (and confusing) hybrids I ever encountered was a Common Goldeneye x Hooded Merganser. Structurally, the bird was a goldeneye, but the plumage (and narrow bill) harked to male Hooded Merganser.

Much recent attention has been given to a rash of bill deformities in birds—i.e., birds showing grotesquely long, curved, even overlapping bills (turning many species into pseudo-crossbills).

But in the field, actual physical abnormalities are less commonly encountered than are plumage or structural changes caused by external circumstances or our powers of perception. In cold weather, birds commonly fluff up, making them appear plumper than normal. When temperatures fall below freezing, yellowlegs often draw their long, trailing legs up close to the body, dramatically altering the typically slender flight profile. When birds are wet or sodden, they often appear darker than normal.

Our perception of a bird's color and even size can be altered by light and background, too. An adult Herring Gull illuminated by full sunlight will show a typical pale gray mantle. But one turned obliquely, so that some sunlight is now reflected away, not toward the observer, will appear a shade or two darker, dark enough for the bird to be mistaken for a Lesser Black-backed Gull.

Against a bright blue sky, American Kestrels look typically tiny. Framed against a dark, overcast sky, they appear, to our eye, abnormally large—large enough for this small falcon to be mistaken for a peregrine at first glance.

Birds with white underparts flying over blue swimming pools take on a blue cast. The white underparts of a Broad-billed Hummingbird perched at a red plastic hummingbird feeder turn pink. In the first light of morning, when the sun is just cresting the horizon, the pale underparts of birds appear yellow.

You are probably feeling an ugly element of uncertainty creeping into your soul right about now, wondering whether any identification made in the field can be counted on to be correct.

Actually, that is a very good question—one that goes all the way back to the origin of field identification and right to the heart of birding.

Take heart in this. Exceptions to the rule are just that, exceptional. You are far, far more likely to encounter typical birds under typical conditions in your forays afield. Exceptions to the rule qualify, they do not undermine, the basic principle that is the foundation of birding.

The Path Less Followed

I lied again, or at least diminished the truth. Early on, I said that the link between where a bird is and where it is supposed to be is only slightly less immutable than the link between what it is and how it appears.

It's time to tell you that sometimes this is not the case, too. Birds do sometimes wander outside of their normal ranges, and they do, sometimes, turn up in habitats where they do not belong. But . . .

Just like anomalies associated with appearance and perception, birds that turn up where they are not commonly found are the exception, not the norm. In fact, this penchant for birds to wander

Bird do sometimes occur in habitat that is not typical, as this beach-loving adult male Red-winged Blackbird attests. (Note: Just outside the image is tidal marsh, classic habitat for this species.)

adds an exciting element to birding, and it is a key component of population dynamics. So while you can rely on most bird species to be where they are supposed to be, when they are supposed to be there, just know that some small number of birds can likewise be counted on to take the path less followed.

This penchant for waywardness is more pronounced in some species than in others and more common at certain times of years than other times.

Birds that are year-round residents, have limited ranges, and/or are tied to very specific habitats tend not to wander. A good example is Brown-headed Nuthatch, a bird of southeastern pine forests that breeds as far north as Lewes, Delaware. Only twice has the bird been seen in Cape May, New Jersey, which lies a mere twelve miles away (but across the Delaware Bay).

On the other hand, some species are very prone to wander outside their normal range, especially those that undergo extensive migrations, are gifted fliers, or routinely relocate in order to exploit unpredictable food resources.

A good example is the Western Kingbird, a bird whose breeding range falls (for the most part) west of the Mississippi River but who nevertheless regularly wanders east of the Mississippi during spring, and especially fall, migration. Another example is Wood Stork, a resident of the southeastern states that has been recorded in almost every state (even north to the Yukon). Periodic drought in its normal range gives this fish-eating bird of shallow waters the impetus to wander. Its ability to use thermals for lift and glide great distances gives it the latitude to travel great distances.

Something to note: Birds that break the range barrier rules are still subject to certain principles. Most vagrancy occurs during migration, especially fall, when many bird species are engaged in a wholesale geographic relocation. Why especially fall? In fall, bird populations are bolstered by a crop of juvenile birds—which are, just like young of our own species, more likely to wander.

Something else to note: Even when birds cross the line geographically, they still maintain a high degree of fidelity to proper habitat. Western Kingbirds that wander to the east still forage in open areas that offer hunting perches (shrubs, trees, fences, utility lines, and barbed wire fences). Wood Storks hundreds of miles out of range still seek out shallow, often muddy, bodies of water—sloughs and ponds.

When birds can't find proper habitat, they do the best they can. Many years ago, David Sibley was birding the residential community of Cape May Point when he heard a call note that reminded him of, in fact, sounded exactly like, a Rock Wren—a bird found, as the name implies, in rocky habitat, west of the American prairies. Cape May Point's substrate is sand, not rock. David found New Jersey's only record of Rock Wren foraging amid the lumber scraps and piled building materials of a home under construction, where, in fact, the bird spent the winter.

Birds found wholly out of habitat are very rare, but even here, these mismatches are not devoid of rhyme or reason. I once flushed an American Coot, a waterbird, from a rocky knoll atop the forested Kittatiny Ridge in New Jersey. The migrating bird had evidently been forced to land the night before, and the open plateau was more inviting to this bird of open water than the surrounding forest.

On another occasion, in the Pawnee National Grassland of Colorado, I flushed a hen pintail from her nest situated in the middle of a cactus patch. The nest was, however, about two hundred feet from a raised metal water tank serving the needs of thirsty cattle.

As for the Black Rail found walking around the downtown shopping district in Cape May by my friend and coworker Patty Hodgetts . . . well, this bird was really lost. On the other hand, the encounter did occur at night, and Black Rails are mostly nocturnal.

Sometimes birds wander outside their prescribed ranges. While maps show Western Kingbird's range falling west of the Mississippi, a few birds regularly wander east as far as the Atlantic Coast in fall and, occasionally, spring.

10 | The End of Field Identification

Since we're being honest with each other, this might be a good time to tell you that almost everything that I have just told you may well be heading for the avocational dustbin. In the not-too-distant future, identifying real birds in real time will likely be about as needful as knowing how to adjust a carburetor or change a typewriter ribbon.

Image capture is destined to revolutionize bird identification—in fact, it already has. A growing number of new birders are entering the hobby through the viewfinders of cameras instead of the lenses of binoculars. What's more, a growing number of experienced birders are bringing cameras, more than their binoculars and skills, to bear when confronted by uncommon or confusing species, changing the very principle of field identification.

A couple years ago, in late September, I was standing with a group of very skilled birders on "the dike" north of Higbee Beach in Cape May. It is a celebrated junction for watching hordes of migrating songbirds engaging in a phenomenon called "morning flight"—a period of relocation, beginning at sunrise, when migrating birds seek out the habitat that meets their needs. It is also the frontier of field identification. A place where birders push the limits of their skills as they strive to pin names to small, darting forms in flight.

On this morning, a bird flying overhead caught everyone's attention but defied recognition. My first impression, based on its shape (long wings, fairly robust bill) and overall yellowish base color, was "female or juvenile Scarlet Tanager."

But it appeared too small for a tanager. It also seemed somewhat dark chested, bibbed.

The brain is an amazing mechanism, and with these clues, bolstered by some ingrained sense of overall shape, and tempered by probability, a name sprang to mind. After a qualitative double check to see if the name did indeed fit the bird, I blurted out: "Yellow-bellied Flycatcher."

It was a good guess. But it was wrong.

Several observers armed with fast-shooting autofocus cameras captured the bird in flight. What the images showed was not Yellow-bellied Flycatcher but the slightly larger Acadian Flycatcher.

Where I went wrong with my identification was not giving more weight to my initial impression of size (Acadian Flycatcher is slightly closer in size to a tanager than is Yellow-bellied) and also by ignoring the fact that Acadian Flycatchers also appear bibbed.

Why I went wrong was, in part, because my decision was skewed by probability. Acadian Flycatchers are early to mid-August migrants in Cape May; Yellow-bellied are more likely in September. Also, encounters with Acadian Flycatcher commonly occur within forest interior. Yellow-bellied is more likely to be found along open edge. While neither flycatcher commonly engages in morning flight, open edge is closer to open sky than forest interior is. My mind made the logical link.

The camera, and subsequent study of the captured image, did what my skill did not: correctly identify the bird. Images in the hand, like study skins in a drawer, are impervious to probability.

There are, today, telephones that take better pictures than the finest wildlife photographer could have taken with the most expensive equipment back when I started birding. In the future, digital imaging systems will be a standard feature of binoculars and spotting scopes, and it won't be long before there will be commercial bird-identification programs that will take these captured images, analyze them, and pin the name to the bird.

Binoculars were the instrument that spurred the art of field identification—i.e., the identification of living birds, in the field, in real time. The camera may signal its end. It is now common practice for bird records committees to require photo documentation to support rare bird sightings (particularly in the case of new state records), and for very tricky identifications, many skilled birders now get the picture first, then certify the identification by studying the image after the fact.

So here, in the early years of the twenty-first century, bird identification is on the verge of coming full circle. It started by collecting birds and identifying them in the hand, after the fact. It has returned to collecting the images of birds, and identifying them in the hand, after the fact.

The art of field identification, the use of human powers of mind and perception to identify real birds in real time, may, in the end, prove to be no more than a passing fad.

Is this a bad thing? Not necessarily. Not if bird identification is regarded as a science instead of an art—a search for verifiable fact instead of a challenge to master with skill.

Me? I think that the very thing that makes field identification compelling, even addicting, is the element of fallibility. If an identification cannot be wrong, it also can never be right. It can only be what is: a fact—devoid of the human element that turns an academic exercise into an art and an engaging hobby enjoyed by millions.

One of these millions is you.

Last Thoughts?

Two.

Insofar as bird watching is a hobby, it presumes that you are doing it for your enjoyment. Yes, bird identification is challenging. Yes, it can be frustrating. But without challenge and frustration there would be no balancing sense of achievement when you master a difficult identification or find a bird you have long aspired to see.

We're a funny species, we humans. We're at our best when we aspire to things just beyond our reach. And since you have read all the way to the end of this book, one of the things you very plainly aspire to be is a better birder.

As you grow in skill, keep this in mind. Birding is first and foremost an activity that is supposed to be fun. It's a hobby—a game, and a low-stakes game at that. The worst thing that can happen is that you misidentify a bird. Nations don't fall. Currencies don't collapse. Children don't starve.

As I love to point out, the difference between a beginning birder and an accomplished birder is that, thus far, beginning birders have misidentified very few birds. Accomplished birders have misidentified thousands.

So relax. Have fun. Savor each and every bird you see or hear.

In the end, when you close the covers on the ledger of your life, you will discover that birding's greatest prize lies not in the skills you acquired but in the harvest of memories your life with birds has brought you.

You can start creating those memories this very day. But before you do, I ask you to think back to the beginning of this book and what I told you about the place where the identification process starts. That's right. Habitat.

Bird populations, and human populations, are only as healthy as the environment that supports them. The wealth of birds we enjoy today is a tribute to that environment and all the effort and good decision making that have gone into protecting it.

If bird watching is indeed a game, then priority one becomes protecting the playing field, the planet that supports the players—the birds, and us. Habitat is not only where the identification process starts, it's where our obligation as custodians of the planet begins.

You don't have to be an experienced birder to understand this. You just have to be an intelligent, responsible, and caring one. If everyone takes this imperative to heart, then not only are we assured of having a diversity of birds to enjoy in our lifetimes, but future generations of bird watchers will be able to enjoy this richness and diversity as well.

More Titles by Pete Dunne . . .

PETE DUNNE
The Art of **Bird Finding**

PETE DUNNE
THE ART OF **PISHING**
includes audio CD

10/1/2012

T